The Principle of Unrest

Activist Philosophy in the Expanded Field

Immediations
Series Editor: SenseLab

> "Philosophy begins in wonder. And, at the end, when philosophic thought has done its best, the wonder remains"
> – A.N. Whitehead

The aim of the Immediations book series is to prolong the wonder sustaining philosophic thought into transdisciplinary encounters. Its premise is that concepts are for the enacting: they must be experienced. Thought is lived, else it expires. It is most intensely lived at the crossroads of practices, and in the in-between of individuals and their singular endeavors: enlivened in the weave of a relational fabric. Co-composition.

> "The smile spreads over the face, as the face fits itself onto the smile"
> – A. N. Whitehead

Which practices enter into co-composition will be left an open question, to be answered by the Series authors. Art practice, aesthetic theory, political theory, movement practice, media theory, maker culture, science studies, architecture, philosophy ... the range is free. We invite you to roam it.

The Principle of Unrest
Activist Philosophy in the Expanded Field

Brian Massumi

OPEN HUMANITIES PRESS
London 2017

First edition published by Open Humanities Press 2017
Copyright © 2017 Brian Massumi

This is an open access book, licensed under Creative Commons By Attribution Share Alike license. Under this license, authors allow anyone to download, reuse, reprint, modify, distribute, and/or copy their work so long as the authors and source are cited and resulting derivative works are licensed under the same or similar license. No permission is required from the authors or the publisher. Statutory fair use and other rights are in no way affected by the above. Read more about the license at creativecommons.org/licenses/by-sa/4.0

Chapter 1 originally appeared in Krystian Woznicki and Brian Massumi, *After the Planes: A Dialogue About Movement, Perception and Politics* (Berlin: Diamondpapers, 2017), 77-178. It is reprinted here with revisions.

Chapter 2 originally appeared as a booklet accompanying the DVD *Performance Dialogues 3* – Brian Massumi, filmed interview directed by Adrian Heathfield and Hugo Glendinning as part of the "Performance Matters" project (Goldsmith's University/University of London/University of Roehampton/Live Art Development Agency/UK Arts & Humanities Research Council). 72 min.

Chapter 3 originally appeared in *Inflexions: A Journal for Research-Creation*, "Radical Pedagogies" special issue, 8 (2015): 59-88. It is reprinted here with minor revisions.

Cover Illustration © 2017 Leslie Plumb
Cover Design by Leslie Plumb

Print ISBN 978-1-78542-044-3
PDF ISBN 978-1-78542-045-0

Freely avalble online at:
http://openhumanitiespress.org/books/titles/the-principle-of-unrest

OPEN HUMANITIES PRESS

Open Humanities Press is an international, scholar-led open access publishing collective whose mission is to make leading works of contemporary critical thought freely available worldwide. More at http://openhumanitiespress.org

Contents

1. Capital Moves   7
2. Movements of Thought   72
3. Collective Expression: A Radical Pragmatics   111
   Works Cited   145

1

Capital Moves

Interview with Brian Massumi
by Krystian Woznicki

Krystian Woznicki: Somehow our world works best when everything (people, data, goods, money, etc.) remains in motion. What is this contemporary co-motion all about? In which particular sense is the social, economic and political framework for such a world conditioned by the global expansion of neoliberal capitalism?

Brian Massumi: The world has always been in movement. The study of human prehistory is currently being rewritten in light of new realizations about the rapidity of the movements that brought our ancestors out of Africa and across Europe and Asia, and about the complexity of the migrations, which, it is now realized, included movements of return among all three continents. There is movement everywhere, from as far back as we can see, and nowhere is it linear. There is a restlessness in human history that constantly tangles the lines, so much so as to call into the question the integrity of the species. Interbreeding between modern humans and other human species, Neanderthals, Denisovans, and at least one other whose existence is at only hinted at, has contributed to our genome, and that contribution is now being tied to specific physiological and phenotypic characteristics of human populations.

This may seem a bit off-topic, but it brings up some crucial points. The first is that there is a principle of unrest that traverses human history. It does so in so entangling a way that it calls into question notions of species integrity, let alone racial purity, and fundamentally challenges the concept of identity as something stable that precedes movement and mixing. It challenges us to rethink movement, in order to think differently about those issues, among many others.

We normally think of movement as simple displacement: a change in location. What is in movement is thought of as remaining fundamentally what it was, retaining its identity across the displacement. But as the human entered into entanglements as it moved through history, it underwent changes in its very nature. It underwent qualitative change. Displacement is just the visible trail of qualitative changes in nature. Displacement is not just a shift of place. It's the index of a becoming: movement not just from one spatial location to another, but from one nature-changing entanglement to another. It's always a question of transformation – transformation in relation.

In the movement of relational transformation, the very definition of what moves changes. Identity is ceaselessly overcome in variation. Should we say, then, that the human has always been on the move throughout its history? Or is it more accurate to say that a movement of relational transformation has moved *through* the human? If so, when did that movement of relational transformation begin? It is clear that the "principle of unrest" predates the human – or rather this continuing process of hominization – and runs the full length of evolution, from the beginnings of life. From this perspective, the human is a carrier of a movement of relational transformation, one that swept it up, and sweeps through it.

KW: Talking about human history and human life in that way feels intuitively right to me. Facing the environment or looking at one's body one somehow knows that everything is in flux – without always being able to actually grasp this. That is also why I personally enjoy reading deconstruction or your philosophical writing: You experience the sense of the world as process. But to come back to my initial question: How does movement play out in capitalism?

BM: Capitalism may well be the figure in which the movement I was just describing actually exceeds the human. The neoliberal moment might be thought of as a vector of becoming coming out the far side of our humanity. It is the moment when market mechanisms declared their autonomy, and the economy became a regime of power in its own right. Governments, let alone individual actors, feel they have no choice but to conform to the operating conditions it sets for them. The cutting edge of capitalism is in the financial markets, which have evolved forms of abstract capital so abstruse, contingent, and objectively undecidable that it is impossible to get an effective grip on them. They run according to their own process, and sometimes run away with themselves, periodically crashing and burning. The financialized economy is beyond the human pale: beyond full human comprehension and beyond effective human control. It is a self-driving machine, operating more and more abstractly, with no one in particular at the steering wheel. It was created by the human, but not in its own image, emerging rather as a monstrous offspring that turns back to engulf its maker and drive away with it.

This is what Deleuze and Guattari in *A Thousand Plateaus* describes in terms of "machinic enslavement," presciently describing the neoliberal moment before the fact (1987: 466-473). They speak of the role of the nation-state changing. The state, they say, now functions as a "model of realization" for global capital, or what Guattari liked to call "worldwide integrated capitalism." What they mean is that nation-states can modulate the way the capitalist process falls on their territory, using their borders as a kind of refractive lens, but they cannot be the master of it. At best, they can create zones of relative stability, precariously sheltering their national territory from the worst effects of the "creative destruction" of capital's transformational movements, and redistributing those effects elsewhere. The situation in Greece vis-à-vis Germany and the other more stable economies at the core of the European Union is a case in point. The Greek state is rendered powerless and forced to accept conditions deeply unacceptable to its population in the name of the core stability of the integrated European market.

But this relation is just an internalization within Europe of the imbalance of capitalist power that has defined the dehumanizing relation between the "developed world" and the "developing world" for a long time. The state's humanistic aspirations (social welfare, universal rights, and respect of the person) have become subordinate to the economic "realities." Philosophy declared the humanism supposedly embodied in the modern state dead many decades ago. But it jumped the gun. It is the neoliberal-capitalist realism that pulled the trigger. Bill Clinton's 1992 presidential campaign slogan said it pithily: "it's the economy, stupid." Twenty-five years on, it still is. It has gotten to the point that it seems that many people have concluded that the only possible way around it is actually to install stupidity at the head of the state (candidate Donald Trump's belief that as president he could man-handle the economy with not-so-invisible little hands had pundits' heads swimming).

KW: There is a lot of talk about how the continuous acceleration of the movement of people, data, goods and money seems to further enlarge the crisis of liberal democracy. A variety of observers have pointed out that democractic apparatuses are not up to dealing with the speed of contemporary movements. What is your take on this?

BM: The speed of contemporary movements is indeed a factor, but speed is not adequate as a diagnostic tool. It is inadequate in light of what I was just saying about displacement being the index of a movement of qualitative change. Speed and acceleration are basically displacement concepts. They are quantitative notions referring to the rate of displacement. How many things and different kinds of things are catapulted into circulation by capital, and how fast they turn over, is the tip of the iceberg. The bulk of the issue is that there has been a qualitative change in *how* capitalism's movements move.

KW: What is this qualitative change about?

BM: Capitalism no longer just assembles its products from raw materials and fabricated components, and then launches them into circulation. That scenario assumes a predesigned product, and a meaningful separation between the realm of production and the realm of circulation. Today, those realms have largely collapsed into each other. Contemporary capitalism is increasingly concerned with setting in place the conditions for its products to *emerge*. They are not only made to emerge, but this happens as a by-product of circulation itself. There are many ways this happens. Examples are the feedback loops that have formed between crowdsourcing and the data-mining of internet, cell phone traffic, and credit-card use on the one hand, and product-development and marketing on the other. The network becomes a matrix of emergence for products that do not preexist, but take shape in and through networked circulation. In the ebb and flow, marketing potentials appear like waves cresting on a sea of movements. These are skimmed off, "mined," then concretized as new products to be sold for profit. You could look at the profit generated as embodying a "surplus-value of flow": a yield of added value emerging from the complexity of movements under way, directly as a function of them. Philosophically speaking, capitalism has learned to motorize itself immanently to its own movements.

The epitome of surplus-value of flow is the way the financial markets operate. At that level, surplus-value is produced by leveraging movements of capital, by gaming turnover, by playing the timing of transactions, by second-guessing the trends, without even the need for a concretized product to emerge, but rather purely through abstract, second-order products like derivatives and credit default swaps. It is toward this short-circuiting of production that the center of gravity of the economy has moved, as if in search of a soul: the spirit of capitalism endeavoring to free itself from the body of production. Capital, self-abstracting. The value of the financial sector in the developed economies is now many times greater than the manufacturing sector. Even if the self-abstracting can never be complete, and the articulation of the financial markets to the so-called "real" economy cannot be eliminated, it is highly significant that the balance has shifted and that the effort of capital to levitate itself from the sphere of concrete production has taken on the piloting role.

Another prominent, very different, way in which capitalism has learned to valorize matrices of emergence is through biotechnology. Biotechnology, for its part, doesn't abstract the body away. It abstracts it *into* existence. It descends to the emergent material level of life, the gene, in order to manipulate the potentials of life's rearising. It operates on an infra-corporeal level. Capital, taking body emergently. The infra-corporeal level is a level that is "immanent" to existence: the well-spring from which it emerges like an artesian well feeding the many streams of life. It is the level of potential.

KW: What do you mean by infra?

BM: "Infra-" is a prefix I like to use to refer to the immanent level at which potentials of emergence are found. As my two examples indicate, the immanence of the infra-, and the manner in which it is accessed and to what effect, is highly variable.

An extraction of surplus-value from an infra-level is not a manufacture. Financial surplus-value comes from capital's becoming self-abstracting as a function of its own flow, hoisting itself on its own soulful petards into another realm of its being. Biotechnological reembodiments, for their part, are more grown than manufactured – they are less made than made to take form, by manipulating how potentials come to express *themselves*. On the infra-level what is at issue is a veritable becoming, a bringing into determinate existence of something prefigured only on the run, in the upswell of as-yet unformed potential. Modulating or manipulating what comes of this level constitutes an extreme form of power: the power to bring to be; the power to make become; the power to harness qualitative transformation. I call it *ontopower* ("onto" from "ontogenesis," or the process of being's becoming).

KW: You recently published two books which develop the concept: *Ontopower* (2015) and *The Power at the End of the Economy* (2014a). I wonder how this concept of power plays out in our discussion about movement.

BM: I said earlier that the economy has become a regime of power in its own right. What I meant is that the capitalist process has made itself an ontopower. This has far-reaching implications for liberal democracy when you consider that according to theorists of neoliberalism, its most astute proponents as well as its critics, neoliberalism does not just produce objects, but also its own subjects. Foucault called the neoliberal subject the "subject of interest," emphasizing that its form is homologous to that of the enterprise. The founding theorists of neoliberalism called this enterprise-subject "human capital." In *The Power at the End of the Economy* and *Ontopower*, I try to look at some of the consequences of the way in which capitalism's ontopower extends to the production of the very capitalized individuals, the capital life-forms, that populate its field. The fact that capitalism has found ways to productively access matrices of emergence means that it now increasingly functions at the *infra-individual* level wherever capital flows – which is everywhere. Capital seeps down to the affective level of felt potential, before life potentials have concretized in a determinate form of life, where life is as-yet emergent.

This level is stirring with micromovements. I call these formative, but not yet fully formed movements "bare activity." With respect to the infra-human, these are ebbs and flows of desire, tendency, fear, hope, self-interest, sympathy, tensings for action and easings into relation. It is as easy as click-bait to modulate that ebb and flow in order to orient its taking-determinate-form. Facebook demonstrated this with its infamous informal experiment in modulating people's moods and online behavior by modulating the affective tenor of their Facebook feeds. Capitalism has learned to descend to the infra-level where the individual is emergently divided among potential inflections of its own self-formative movements. Deleuze coined a word for the neoliberal subject, taking this self-dividing, this "schizzing," into account: the "dividual" (Deleuze 1995).

My hypothesis is that neoliberal capitalism directly couples this infra-individual level with the transindividual level. It energizes itself with feedback effects between the infra- and transindividual levels in a way that largely bypasses the intermediate level of the supposedly self-contained individual. This intermediate level is that of the social or moral person: the figure of the citizen, as subject of right, and the subject of rational interest. This level of the person, at which we like to think we function, is reduced to a hinge mechanism through which the infra- and the trans- communicate: a miniaturized "model of realization" of global capital, zoomed down to fit the contours of the human body (or rather, the pattern of whole-body movements indexing the flow of a quantum of human-capital becoming). The transindividual level is, at its widest horizon, the integrated worldwide network of qualitatively transformational movements whose complexity and contingency escapes not only individual human control, but mastery by any individual nation-state.

KW: If the figure of the citizen is somehow suspended in capitalism, what does that imply for models of democracy?

BM: There is a fundamental misfit between the multi-scale regime of ontopower I just described and liberal democracy. Liberal democracy is ostensibly predicated on the personal sanctity of the individual subject of right, the citizen safely enwrapped within the sovereign sanctity of the individual state. Liberal democracy only knows how to work across those two scales of individuality, the fully formed citizen and the sovereign state (neither of which is what it purports to be any longer). Its bridging strategy is the mechanism of representation. It is this mechanism that has broken down.

Representation is dead – if it was ever really alive. Who today feels truly represented by their elected government? Witness the exodus from the established parties throughout the world, most vividly illustrated by the rise of the populist "independent" voter in the United States and elsewhere who disavows any party allegiance that would inscribe them in the institutionalized, normative functionings of their supposedly representative governmental system. The result is a simultaneous leakage from the left and the right, producing an increasing polarization. The mechanism of representation is obsolete. It assumes a stable identity on both scales: a government that mirrors who its citizens are, and citizens who embody the identity of the state, in a mutually structuring embrace. The prevailing conditions, however, are of continual qualitative change, ceaseless transformational relational movements – as far from a stable structure as you can get. The structural embrace has been swept through by becoming, transversed by flows that are increasingly uncontrolled by anyone or any one institution in particular.

As a result, the purportedly rational intercourse liberal democracy assumes as the necessary condition for its structure of representation has been swamped by affect stirred up by the structurally disavowed instability. Affective tides ebb and flow. In their upswell they prefigure emergent, far-from-equilibrium follow-on movements whose direction is increasingly unpredictable. Representation lies among the flotsam and jetsam like a weather-beaten plastic bottle.

KW: Could you give an example?

BM: Look at the Brexit vote. UK voters voted to "take back their country" from the supra-national EU, but the complexity of the situation actually means that what they may get is their country's breaking apart, with Scotland now reconsidering its own recent vote to stay in the union. They voted to represent their perceived personal and national interests, only to be taken aback by the result, leading to a widespread expression of hand-wringing contrition the very next day, out of sudden doubt that their representation of their interests represented their interests. A resounding decision of indecision.

The whole thing was an exercise in the avoidance of the political crux of the matter: that non-representative forms of democracy need to be invented, at the interpersonal, national, and supra-national levels – or better, transversal to them all, in a new kind of infra-trans feedback system yet to be invented. Playing the identity card and the associated discourse of particularist interest, on whatever level, leads nowhere. The plastic bottle of representation, half-full of polluted water, is running on empty. The dividual rules – one way or another. The dividual is the individual divided among itself. This considerably complicates the calculus of interests, which become undecidable within the structure of representation. Perhaps, if new practices are invented for it, rather than in denial of it as is presently the case, the dividual can become the seat of ontopowers counter to capital: counter-ontopowers.

KW: Where to start?

BM: It is important, in thinking about what democracy could become, to try to theorize this becoming integrally-affective of politics and the role of the dividual. This has to be done without giving credence to the idea that rationality and affectivity are opposites (rather, deconstructing that opposition). It is critical to be able to think about and experiment with the ways in which affectively-based politics can give rise to radically inclusive forms of direct democracy.

KW: The term direct democracy is often used to refer to referenda.

BM: Yes, but as Brexit has shown once again, in the networked, affectively energized political environment, the referendum is but a caricature of it. Prefigurative glimpses of what it could be have been seen in the spontaneously self-organizing movements of the 2010s, from Occupy and the *indignados* forward through events like 2016's Nuit Debout, and their power of contagion across identity lines. Nothing like a definitive model has emerged. But something has been stirring. The politics-to-come will likely have no definitive model, by dint of transformative movement. No one model, but many relational matrices, in resonance and interference. That prospect is uncertain, even unsettling, but the alternative is downright frightening: a return of a kind of affective politics more akin to the one whose ravages we know only all too well from the history of the twentieth century – the radically exclusive anti-democratic movements of fascism. These also are stirring, in the same cauldron of bare activity, immanent to the same field of complexity.

KW: How could we reimagine and rebuild democracies by understanding movement better?

BM: As a preliminary to that question, it is important to think very hard about the historical conjuncture we have arrived at. If a vector of becoming has swept through and come out the far side of the human adventure in the form of the neoliberal-capitalist machinery of ontopower, then the label of the Anthropocene to designate the age we are entering is off the mark. I find Jason W. Moore's term the "Capitalocene" (Moore 2015) a much better starting point, because this is the age in which the movement of the capitalist process through the human outstrips "man," precisely by making the effects of "his" activity ubiquitous, in ever more complicated feedback effects between levels that escape his control, to the ultimate detriment of his own life environment and, potentially, his very survival.

To a certain extent, this dovetails with the discourse of what has come to be known as accelerationism. But we have to be careful. It is necessary to work through the issues guided by an understanding of movement as qualitative transformation. The premise of accelerationism is that capitalism's natural tendency is to speed things up. Since the mobilization of capital is now ubiquitous, the only way out is to encourage it to speed up its own speeding up ever more. In catastrophist versions, the acceleration will reach a point where the capitalist economy can no longer catch its own tail in surplus-value of flow, and it falls in a heap – the crisis to end all capitalist crises. All of this is couched in quantitative terms of speed.

KW: Yes, we touched upon this issue already.

BM: It's crucial to return to that point here, in order to account for the possibility – I would call it a certainty – that in the field of emergence plied by the movements of capitalism there are emergent potentials for qualitatively different modes of existence that are stultified because –if they were allowed to take fully formed expression, if the budding tendencies they prefigure were to deploy and express themselves to their fullest power – they would move in directions beyond capitalism's orbit. In other words, on the infra-level of potential there are germinal stirrings of counter-powers of emergence. These are ontopowers immanent to capitalism's processual field, but as-yet uncaptured by its logic. When movements suddenly and inexplicably erupt, as happened in 2010-2011 and sporadically since, in one country after another, it is these potentials germinating and coming to a paroxysmal expression that suddenly calls everything into question, at times extending to capitalism itself, only to fizzle just as quickly they came. If we honed ways of understanding these countertendencies, perceiving them in germ, curating the traces of their passing in a way that makes them reactivatable, then perhaps we could coax them into taking more enduring form – or at least iterating more often, with more transformational relational overlaps, and as a result greater potential for contagion. Perhaps it is possible to extract counter-capitalist surplus-values of movement.

If this is possible, it is only by acting directly in the register of affect. No amount of ideological analysis or persuasion will do the trick, because programmatic politics is as implicated in structures of representation and identity as liberal democracy is, although from a different angle (for example, in the guise of the "will of the people" as spear-headed by a vanguard, explicitly or in the implicit form of a technocratic elite). The counter-tendencies I'm talking about are just as moving, just as emergent and, ultimately, just as self-driving as the machine of capitalism itself – only with a different, non-monetary, directly qualitative sense of value. That is a sense of the value of movements, events, relations, in and for themselves, a sense of aliveness, the sense of intensity that comes with the experience of potential. These unmonetizable surplus-values of movement feedback into themselves, in their own currency of experienced potential, sketching alter-economies of transformational relation. They are tendentially anti-capitalist counter-ontopowers immanent to the capitalist field.

KW: I am not sure I can follow your interest in value.

BM: The call to focus on the question of the qualitative in movement is a proposal to return to the question of value, radically rethought outside programmatic politics or normative ethics. To concede the question of value to capitalism, moralism, or conformism is to lose the battle before it begins. Any democracy-to-come will arrive as a collective embodiment of emergent intensities of experience whose living-out *is* its own value, immanent to that live event, before they are encasted in any institutional armature, and with the tendency to push across and overspill any regularizing or regulatory incorporation, in a perpetual cycle of stabilizing capture and revivifying escape.

This is value not unlike the way in painting we speak of the value of a color. This is where I want to take my work next: toward a rethinking of politics based on a chromatic theory of value (Massumi 2017). The basis for a chromatic politics can be found in the work of Whitehead and Ruyer, and in a unique formulation in the work of Fred Moten (although Moten would have serious reservations about rehabilitating the term value).

KW: Activism and emancipatory politics in general are often searching for the outside to capitalism. The way you linked capitalism and movement, the question arises: Is there an outside to movement? In a world that is centered around movement, is even non-movement a type of movement?

BM: No, there is no outside to movement. As Erin Manning points out in her book *Relationscapes* (2009), even stillness is composed of movements. Standing still is a dynamic balance achieved through liminally perceptible micromovements of muscles and attention. In physics, the vacuum is abuzz with dark energy and teams with cosmic rays. As Bergson maintained, there is no such thing as immobility. There are only regimes of movement of qualitatively different kinds whose manners of combining and disjoining compose motional-relational fields. Objects are coagulations of these fields: motional-relational knots that come to stand out as saliencies against the background activity from which they arise and which continues to sustain them for as long as they endure: objects are movement field-effects. The same could be said of situations and events, and even logics (which always arise from and express themselves through patterns of movement).

Given everything I've been saying about movement and capitalism, the way in which the question regarding the outside to capitalism is answered determines a great deal about what kind of anti-capitalist politics makes sense – or if any anti-capitalist politics of the activist variety makes sense. This question is emphatically raised by the recent debates around accelerationism.

An attitude that sometimes comes with perspectives related to accelerationism is that since capitalism is all about mobilization, any move we make is just feeding its logic. A related position sometimes arises from a reading of Giorgio Agamben's thesis that the greatest power is the power not-to, since to-do is to collapse the wave packet of potential into a limited expression of it. This can lead to the conclusion that the most powerful action is non-action. This has led in some quarters to a critique of activism that dovetails with certain attitudes that could be reinforced by accelerationism. For if capitalism is all about mobilization, then to make a move is just to feed its logic further, so why even try to make counter-moves? We are all in capitalism's movement, which is now gone global and become universal.

KW: There is no outside of capitalism, it is said.

BM: The only option, then, is to let, or encourage, the movements of capitalism push themselves to the point of no return. This is an interesting position, but it ignores the qualitative points I started out with: not only are there qualitatively different kinds of movement, but movement as displacement is but the visible index of qualitative variation. It also presupposes certain ideas about the nature of capitalism. To say that there is no outside of capitalism so that everything we do is "inside" it, is implicitly to construe it as a structure: a set of interacting elements whose functioning delineates a bounded space of operation. The accelerationist will counter that the point is just the opposite: capitalism operates in the unbounded space of its own universality, and that is precisely why everything we do is in it. But this riposte is based on a logical flaw.

KW: Could you elaborate on that?

BM: Well, I agree that capitalism is unbounded and there is no getting outside of it, and that it is universal in that sense, but when I say that I mean it very differently, in a way that doesn't entail the conclusion that everything we do is "in" it. The logical question is: How can you say that a space without boundaries is an interiority? Is not a space without boundaries rather a *field of exteriority*? A great outside: an expanded field. If the capitalism's field of operation is a field of exteriority, then we have to invert the question. Given that everything is afoot in a great outside, under what circumstances can we say that *anything* is inside? Deleuze and Guattari answer: when mechanisms deploy themselves to contain it. When it is *captured* by a system or structure and folded into it, incorporated into it. The capitalist field is full of what Deleuze and Guattari call "apparatuses of capture" (1987: 424-473). There are prisons, schools, legal systems, bureaucracies, political parties, corporations, nongovernmental organizations, all manner of institutions and quasi-institutions. Each sets its own operative boundaries in order to set itself apart. The setting-apart allows for an internal logic proper to that domain to hold sway inside the boundaries of that territory.

To say that these formations are "capitalist" is not untrue, but it is not sufficient, since each also has its own operating logic.

They must of course bend to the logic of capital. They are fed by capital and under neoliberalism are allowed to prosper only if they in turn feed the capitalist economy, providing something that can be considered an "added value" for it. Under neoliberalism, the raison d'être of everything is justified in economic terms. Even so, these formations are not simply "capitalist." A for-profit prison in the United States is capitalist – but it is still also carceral. It participates in two logics, capitalism and carcerality. Overall, it answers to a fuzzy logic: one that allows for partial belonging in more than one set.

Being "in" capitalism is a question of *degrees of inclusion* in its field. "Degrees" might still imply a quantitative distinction, but what I'm getting at is a qualitative difference: different, interacting logics corresponding to qualitatively different modes of relation. A for-profit prison feeds off of flows of capital. But it also feeds off of flows of criminality. The flows of criminality answer to a logic of infraction implying modes of relation that are not outside capitalism, but are not reducible to the capitalist relation. Each such logic constitutes its own mode of relation corresponding to a qualitatively different degree of inclusion in the neoliberal fold. The model is of symbiosis: formations that are incorporated in a larger assemblage and serve its global logic, but at the same time retain a certain heterogeneity.

KW: Can you say more about the way in which carcerality and criminality are not reducible to the capitalist relation?

BM: Marx defines capitalist relation as a conjunction between a flow of labor-power and a flow of money as salary, cross-cut by a flow of commodities and a flow of money as means of payment. Each conjunction presents itself as an equal exchange, value for value, as measured by money in yet another guise, as general equivalent. In reality, the exchange is unequal. The capitalist relation is actually predicated on an asymmetry: profit. An excess is skimmed off, and channeled into yet another form of money:

investment money. Technically, capital is not the quantity of profit, but rather the ability of investment money to produce an increased quantity of money in the future. That increase-over any present quantity of money, already present in investment potential, is capitalist surplus-value.

It is interesting to note here that the capitalist relation is essentially a *time-form*, and that as a time-form its native tense is the future. Now, a for-profit prison bathes in the capitalist relation. It participates in it on all sides, including on the inside. It lives for the capital flows it captures and channels into surplus-value production. But it also captures flows of criminality and channels them into a different form of surplus-value production: a surplus-value of social order, of normalization. Or at least, it produces as a surplus-value the affects associated with these, even if the ends of social order and normalization are not actually met. Which they aren't. At any rate, the disciplinary logic of normalization is not specifically capitalist. It is found in many kinds of society. I would go so far as to argue that it doesn't correspond to the actual direction in which the logic of neoliberalism preferentially moves. The watchword of neoliberalism is not "conform," but rather "excel": exceed the norm. Its call is to "innovate": reinvent the norm. The direction of movement is toward the supernormal. The very idea that there is a normal situation has gone out the window. The situation is understood to be complex, if not chaotic, and the job of the business executive or entrepreneur is to learn how to creatively depart from normal operating procedures in order to make a peerless leap that seizes upon the singularity of the situation – rather than confirming and conforming to a notion of its regularity. I do not agree with critiques of present-day capitalism that lament its homogenizing effects. Its logic embraces heterogeneity, and fosters it, on the condition that the resulting variation remain within the orbit the capitalist relation. From this point of view, the ostensibly normalizing function of the prison might be seen as a compensatory mechanism for the supernormal disruptiveness of capitalism's logic: a calmative balm for the harried voter. This might be a useful defense mechanism for capitalist business as usual, but that does not change the fact that the its logic is different from the logic that of the capitalist relation as such.

As Foucault made abundantly clear in *Discipline and Punish* (1977), the carceral system actually produces more of the criminality that it is its stated objective to stamp out, rather than effectively normalizing the population as it ostensibly purports to do. In my work on preemption, I assert that this positive production of what is supposed to be negated is a characteristic of all preemptive mechanisms of power. This aspect of the disciplinary institution prefigures ontopower, whose power to bring to be, I argue, revolves around preemption. But the main point for the moment is that the for-profit prison, as disciplinary institution, has its own logic, which is not reducible to the capitalist relation without remainder, and that it also feeds off modes of relation that are likewise irreducible to the capitalist without remainder. In this case, what is fed upon is criminality, of which the prison's dedicated institutional logic of carcerality is a function. Of course, much criminal activity is conducted for profit, and criminal organizations have a kind of entrepreneurial spirit. But not all crimes are for profit. The spectrum of criminality extends into other territories (in particular, territories of passion). The equation between criminality, carcerality, and capitalism is far from perfect. There is co-functioning, but there are also areas of disjunction and relative autonomy. The more useful model, again, is symbiosis, rather than hegemony, if hegemony is understood to imply a single dominant structure sucking everything in without remainder and making everything homogeneous (or at least homologous). Symbiosis, but also parasitism.

Repeat this analysis, based on degrees of inclusion and relative autonomy, for every institution or quasi-institution cohabiting the contemporary field of capitalist life. You then get the image of a field that is bathed through and through with the capitalist relation, but also *rife with other modes of relation* that are capturable by different apparatuses, and channeled by each toward a dedicated form of surplus-value whose production fuels the apparatus in question, driving it forward into its own future operations. This self-driving of each apparatus describes a tendency: a way of orienting to the future. Now consider that institutions and quasi-institutions are historically emergent, and that capitalist society is highly conducive to their emergence, multiplication, and differentiation – what is referred to as its "pluralism" and, rightly or wrongly, identified with the representative form of government originating with the nation-states of the capitalist center.

KW: What is your conclusion?

BM: The idea is that the capitalist field is rife with tendencies embodying relations that cannot be reduced to the capitalist relation itself. It is not only rife with them, they are constantly self-multiplying and differentiating – leading to the corresponding multiplication and differentiation of the apparatuses dedicated to their capture and their channeling into institutional and quasi-institutional self-drivings. Each mechanism of capture piggy-backs on an emergent tendency. Some of the emergent tendencies are symbiotic only as a ruse, or as a first camouflaged move toward a fuller expression. If that expression were to be taken to its logical conclusion, the resulting movement would fully realize other values than capitalist value, and would inevitably become antagonistic to capitalism itself. These tendencies are parasites in the pores of the body of capitalist society. They originate as adventitious growths.

You could even say that *every* tendency arising in the capitalist field is adventitious to the extent that it affirms itself: to the extent that experiences its own coming to pass as a value in

[handwritten note at top: "Friendship as method / Publishing chapt"]

itself, independently of the monetary value that it may attributed to it. Such tendencies are passional: that is the best word for a movement that affirms its own occurring. Love is a good example, as long as the analogy is not taken too far, since the kinds of tendencies I'm talking about come in many an affective form – we're back at the affective level I talked about earlier. Love is tied up with all manner of economic pressures and opportunities, but we still seek and sustain it for its own sake. We value it for its own quality, for the heightening of experience it brings: for the qualitative surplus-value it offers. For neoliberal economists, this kind of noncapitalist surplus-value is a problem. Its affirmation may well lead a person, in the name of "quality of life," to resist the role of "human capital" that neoliberalism assigns to them. Human capital is the idea, foundational to neoliberalism, that human life not only serves the capitalist relation, but that it *is* a form of capital: that everyone's basic "job," which we are hired into simply by virtue of being born, is to be an "entrepreneur of oneself": to make every decision, including how one spends one leisure time, including what kind of affective alliances to enter into, based on how it will optimize one's competitiveness, increase one's market value, in order to yield the maximum monetizable return in the future.

The capitalist field is swarming with non-capitalist tendencies. These are to some extent aided and abetted by neoliberal capitalism's own supernormal tendency, which opens the pores wider than normal, creating elbow room for adventitious tendencies following a different logic. Everything possible is done to bring these tendencies into the fold. They are articulated with the capitalist relation by the apparatuses of capture that feed off them. But there is always a remainder, a left-over of bare activity passionally agitating the capitalist field. You could even say that the fundamental antagonism of capitalism under neoliberalism, at least as fundamental as class, is the antagonism between monetized, capitalist surplus-value and noncapitalist, purely qualitative surplus-value – what I call surplus-value of life.

You can think of the capturing institutions and quasi-institutions in the way I was talking about objects in relation to movement earlier: motional-relational knots that come to stand out as saliencies against the background activity from which they arise, and which continues to sustain them for as long as they endure; as movement field-effects which come to stratify the field of life.

That is: life's field of exteriority. The emergent tendencies are brought into the fold, and take on a contributing function. In themselves – that is to say, in their own adventitious emergence – they are uncontained. They are emergently *outside*. Their agitation forms a great outside of emergence, understood not in a spatial sense, but in the processual sense of bare, background activity, arising, in-coming, passionally, out of immanence. The formations they feed into demarcate the inside of capitalism, understood as a complex array of interacting structures and systems, each of which is a relative outside to the others, and all of which together, in their interactions and reciprocal standing apart, distinguish themselves from the great outside of bare, tendential activity.

KW: Speaking of capitalism as an array of systems somehow suggests a degree of stability and order that one hardly can call a reality when facing today's neoliberal mess of uncertainties.

BM: That's right. We need more than a concept of system. When we say the "capitalist system" what we are designating is this tangle of insides reciprocally limiting each other with their respective external boundaries and regimes of passage across their thresholds. But capitalism is more than that. More than a system, or even a system of systems or structure of structures, it is a *process*. A system is defined by its operational closure. A structure is defined by its functional parameters. A process is in touch with a great outside. It is defined by its openness to that great outside: by how it dips into and captures the tendential potentials stirring there. These potentials are unlimited – they are always astir, ready to offer more of themselves. Rather than any in-itself of things, we're talking about the *of-itself* of the world, the giving-of-itself of the world's potential, the partitive, parturitional movement of formative activity, not yet fully channeled into taking determinate form.

A process is unbounded – but limited. It is limited by its ability to dip into the unlimited of the great outside. This reserve of bare activity that it verges on is its *immanent limit*. This is a way of saying that the capitalist process, as apparatus of capture of monetary surplus-value in symbiosis with any number of institutions and quasi-institutions sharing its field, is paradoxically *limited by potential*. Capitalism is continually pushing its immanent limit further by finding more and more ways to redescend to the emergent level of the world's movements. Earlier I mentioned some of the ways this happens: biotechnology, affect, and what I called surplus-value of flow, the extraction of surplus-value purely as a movement-effect. The extraction of surplus-value of flow is always resonant with affect, whether on Facebook or in the financial markets, which are like mood rings of fear and anticipation. Still, even in the face of these ontopowers, the continual giving-of-itself of potential outstrips the capacity of capitalism, and its fellow-traveling institutions, to capture it and channel it to their own ends. There is always a remainder: an excess of potential over capture, of bare activity over useful function, of just-arising over normalized operation. If you define action in terms of functionality or operativity, then there is always an *excess of activity over action*. In Deleuze and Guattari's vocabulary, there are always "lines of flight" suggesting themselves: tendential movements which, if extended to follow their own arc, uncaptured, would move in very different directions than the established channels: these are the counter-ontopowers I mentioned earlier.

KW: What does this mean with respect to the question of whether there is an outside to capitalism and, if not, whether our every move is "in" it?

BM: It means that there is a surfeit of potentials that are *immanent to capitalism's field but not inside its system*. There is always an excess of activity afoot that has not been mobilized into action. There is always an excess of potentials (*puissances*) suggesting themselves but are not yet channeled into the exercise of powers (*pouvoirs*). There is no outside of capitalism in the sense that, in its tireless displacement of its immanent limit, there is nowhere it cannot go potentially. It is virtually everywhere. The attractor of the capitalist relation is tendentially space-filling. It is by nature imperialistic. It is universal by vocation. Processually speaking, however, it is awaft in a great outside of bare activity. It is hard to describe the "exteriority" of this field of germinal life, because we have no words for a nonspatial domain. As it is used here, the word "outside" is directly processual and lacks a spatial connotation, so in a sense it is arbitrary to call it that. We're talking about what Blanchot and Deleuze called an absolute outside, more radically open than any mere exterior defined as such relative to the enclosure of an interior. An immanent outside: the in-which of all that stirs forth.

The distinction between activity and action makes it possible, in fact absolutely necessary, to affirm an activism against capitalism, and suggests that this can be done without automatically falling "into" its fold. This is not to say that is possible for any activity to remain outside it. In the great outside, there are no steady footholds. The absolute outside is a reserve of potential, not a place of refuge to hunker down in. The moment a line of flight begins to draw itself out, it begins to enter the institutional/quasi-institutional landscape. Even if it succeeds in avoiding being captured by a particular formation, it is necessarily navigating the *relative* outside of the cracks between institutions, and that necessity inflects its course. It may also find itself in head-to-head confrontation, in which case it is immediately identified in the terms that particular formation uses to designate its unassimilable outside: enemy, criminal, deviant, refugee, free-loader. This nomination is in itself a partial assimilation, because it influences the arc of the movement of resistance. There is an ineluctable tendency for a counter-ontopowerful movement to fall into some form of complicity.

KW: The question would be whether there is something like emancipatory complicity as opposed to one that is merely catering to dominant ontopowers.

BM: The idea is that complicity is of the nature of things. The idea that everything is included in the capitalist field to a certain degree and that there are degrees of inclusion rather than a simple inside and outside, makes it possible, and necessary, to work with this complicity rather than simply moralizing about it. Work with it – or better, play it. Play with it. Play on it. Game it. *Processual duplicity* is an ontopowerful tool. It is not the same as dishonesty: it is the fuzzy-set capacity of the dividual to truly belong to two sets at the same time, but not in like manner, rather with simultaneous divergent tendencies in co-operation. The practice of processual duplicity is a way, limited by necessity it is true, of prolonging the "schizzing" of bare activity into the institutional landscape – a way of keeping a hold on potential, of continuing to be on the move with a quantum of becoming.

Processual duplicity requires a rethinking of the limits of capitalism. Earlier, I set out some traditional Marxist terms. My definition of the capitalist relation was the basic, textbook Marxist definition. But the concepts started to stray from traditional Marxist vocabulary. For example, traditionally Marxists would say that the limit of capitalism is property. In the schema I have just presented, property is not the absolute *processual limit* of capitalism, which is rather capitalism's trucking with its own immanent outside. Private property is the absolute *systemic limit* of capitalism. What marks a movement's entry into the capitalist system is its gaining the possibility of being designated as property, or of feeding in some way or another the accumulation of property. Property is one of the requisite conditions for the capitalist system, the enterprise-form being another, and quantifiability (the standardization of measure and accounting) yet another (this is not an exhaustive list). The capitalist system is a way of building upon these conditions in combination, in intrication. No one of them in isolation is adequate to its definition as a system. But property is the linchpin. Were the property form to crumble, the capitalist system would surely crumble with it. It might also crumble should one of its co-conditions be withdrawn, in such a way that its removal rebounded upon the property form. Capitalism would have hit its limit as a system. An absolute systemic limit of this kind can be called an *ulterior limit*: a threshold across which the capitalist system falls out of itself. This could conceivably occur from capitalism pushing certain of its *own* movements too far, so that it falls out its own far side – at which point it is swallowed back into its everywhere immanent limit (which, in a topological processual torsion, folds around, the great outside coinciding with the beyond of the far side).

The kinds of institutional and quasi-institutional boundaries populating the field of capitalism that I discussed around the example of the prison are *relative limits*, in contradistinction to the absolute limits, both immanent and ulterior. An anti-capitalist counter-ontopower is one that connects to and prolongs emergent tendencies which, if they were to follow their arc to its logical conclusion, would ultimately lead to the abolition of property as we know it.

It is important to note that anti-capitalist counter-ontopowers have to be defined in relation to both absolute limits at the same time: as a partaking in the potential of bare activity at the immanent limit, and concurrently as a tendency moving through the institutional landscape toward an ulterior limit. You could envision the two types of absolute limit as operating along different coordinate dimensions, one horizontal, at the far end of the line through the history of capitalism vectors (the ulterior limit), and the other vertical, having to do with the field of ontogenetic emergence that infra-infests that history with bare activity at every point along the way, feeding its onward trajectory with potentials that may be capturable but never without remainder, so that they are always also potential lines of escape (the immanent limit).

KW: Financial capital seems to be the prime contemporary example of the very movement of capital threatening to fall out its far side.

BM: Yes. In the form of derivatives called collateralized debt obligations, debts like home mortgages are bundled together and sold as an investment package mixing high- and low-risk debts. This "tranching" is meant to "securitize" the overall product. If the debts composing any particular tranche defaults, the effect of that breakdown is watered down and the overall value is safeguarded. The underlying "assets" (i.e., debts) can be packaged into more than one product: the debt packages can be sold on to other investors, wholly or in part. This multiplies and divides the assets at the same time: it fractalizes them. The complexity can get to the point where who owns what can be impossible to ascertain. The debt then becomes uncollectable. This was one of the contributing factors behind the 2008 financial crisis in the US. In some cases, ownership became indeterminate by dint of an excess of it. Property was threatened by over-ownership. Capitalism's in-built tendency toward excess can be its own worst enemy, leading it to the point where it calls its own systemic requisites into question, in this case property itself.

This is where accelerationist notions might be helpful. It is perhaps possible to identify tendencies toward excess in the way capitalism itself is working, and help push them over the edge of one of its ulterior limits. It is along these lines that accelerationists Alex Williams and Nick Srnicek are thinking, but within a very different theoretical framework (their call for a "Promethean politics of maximal self-mastery over society and the environment" is obviously going in very different directions from the ones I am suggesting; Williams and Srnicek 2014: 360).

From my perspective, the move to accelerate only becomes compelling in light of the kinds of qualitative considerations I have been arguing for, connecting them to the idea of bare activity as the immanent limit of capitalism. The only reason to push capitalism beyond its pale is to allow non-capitalist forms of surplus-value to affirm themselves in the expression of potentials for qualitatively different movements and modes of relation whose value is their own occurrence, whose only justification is their lived quality: what I called a minute ago *surplus-values of life*. Anywhere a non-monetized surplus-value of life is generated there has occurred what I term, again following Deleuze and Guattari, an *escape* to the immanent limit. Escapes can be deviations, perversions, hijacking, hackings. They come in many varieties.

KW: Could you give an example for such escapes developing out of the logic of capitalism?

One example is the open source movement, which hijacks the digitality driving the networking of capitalism toward the production of surplus-values of non-proprietary cooperation: surplus-values of the flow of cooperation. What I am pointing to here relates to property, but perhaps even more directly to another of the ulterior limits of capitalism that I mentioned: quantification; a notion of value that is fundamentally quantitative. Cooperation is immeasurable. It is experienced, qualitatively, as a value in itself. Cooperation is something that is encouraged by neoliberalism in its own service: one of its catchwords is "team work," which has spawned a whole industry of management consulting. But in the case of the open source movement, cooperation is the object of a passional affirmation that can find itself in acute antagonism with property rights.

Another example are the potentials of the blockchain form behind Bitcoin. Bitcoin, and its offspring Ethereum, are runaway speculative forms of capital whose escape was only apparent. They were designed to be convertible into fiat money, and they reproduced many of the same functions underpinning traditional finance: a transactional model in which exchange was the basic social relation; a quantified system of value, enabling exchange to be construed as equal (value for value); a definition of the financial actor as share-holder, preserving private ownership; and all of this within an economy of scarcity (there is a limit to the number of Bitcoin that can be mined). What Bitcoin did was to demonstrate that speculative finance could operate independently of the banks, corporate and sovereign, that are currently at the heart of the financial system, and outside the existing political hierarchies. It gave birth to the "distributed autonomous organization," or DAO. As the blockchain has evolved, the simple transaction model of exchange is being replaced the idea of "smart contracts" that could take any number of forms. Some people are intrigued by the idea that the smart contract could be stretched beyond the traditional economic model, to become the basis for what are essentially social pacts operating according to another logic. This would enable a DAO to prefigure a different economy in miniature.

The research-creation laboratory I work with, the SenseLab, is collaborating with a cooperative called the Economic Space Agency (ECSA) to explore this possibility. ECSA's project is to create an ecology of self-governing DAO-based "economic spaces," each of which would design their own internal cooperative economy to support collective projects. SenseLab's project is to invent affectively charged online modes of operation that foster collective action offline, in a way that is experienced as the creation of a surplus-value of life. There would be a dedicated currency pegged to the qualitative surplus-value of life generated through the back-and-forth between online collaboration and offline events. This special currency – the working name for which is Occurrency – would be convertible to a general ECSA currency, and through it to the other special currencies of the surrounding economic spaces in the shared ecology and even, if desired, to Bitcoin and national currencies. We're working very hard on models for this. Much experimentation is still to be done, and there is no guarantee of success.

One thing that has become clear is that the project will only work if, in our particular collective space of operation, the model of currency is dethroned from its position of centrality. With currency comes the logic of the market, and with that comes an activation of long-ingrained habits and orientations, creating inexorable pressure back towards a primacy of the quantitative and the kinds of individualizing, self-interest-based calculations I just criticized in the case of Bitcoin, no matter how collectivist the intention. It is in fact the logic of the financial markets that offers the most potential for radical reappropriation: the logic of derivatives (Bryan and Rafferty 2006; Lee and Martin 2016).

I talked a bit earlier about the way in which derivatives begin to liquefy the very concept of property. Another aspect of that is that there is no necessity to actually own the underlying asset involved in order to enter into a derivative contract. Neither is there a necessity to actually take ownership at the conclusion of the contract: that is the whole point of options. Whereas a currency pivots on the present instant of exchange, derivatives pivot on futures and allied forms. The future, rather than quantitative equivalence, is their medium. They are speculative by nature, forever deferring. Which means: forever feeding their own movement forward. The absence of a grounding in the solid foundation of an underlying asset of known value, combined with the openness and uncertainty of the perpetual future tense, places affective dynamics all the more intensely at the center, as the motor of the process. If you put all of this together, you can start to imagine a non-ownership-based, self-motoring speculative process "backed" by collectively produced, creatively induced affective intensity: a creative process engine run on the collective generation of surplus-value of life. This is the direction we are trying to go in. Building on a title from one of Guattari's last books (2014), our creative economy will be called the Three Ecologies Process Seed Bank (we had originally named it Adventure Capital, but in the end decided that the neoliberal connotations of that moniker were too strong). The offline events would compose an alternative collective learning environment, a kind of alter-university called the Three Ecologies Institute that the SenseLab would transition into. The point of the economy would be to sustain that project. All of the value generated would be cycled back into it.

Although there would be a currency involved, its operations would be kept peripheral. The intensities coursing through the project would be lived for their own value. Intensity is a double-edged sword: in itself, it marks a purely qualitative difference. At the same time, its fluctuations can be construed as changes in intensive magnitude. This enables it to be translated into quantitative terms: transduced from the realm of quality to the realm of quantity by the application of suitable mechanisms of measure. The transduction renders it comparable, inducts it into a system of equivalence. You just have to think of the irreducible, n-dimensioned singularity of the weather at any given moment, and the inimitable qualitative feel it carries, and then the way that is quantified as a degree of temperature on the thermometer, with its linear scale of units of measure, and by that operation rendered comparable. Our idea is to exploit this transducibility of intensity. The fluctuations of collaborative affective energies running through the project would be treated as a creative climate. At the periphery of the space, mechanisms of measure would be applied which would "take the temperature" of the flow of intensities: unitize it and render it comparable, and therefore convertible. In a word, monetize it. From the point of view of this quantitative translation, the n-dimensioned intensities of the collaborative climate would be flattened into something like a proto-monetary mass. Internally, the qualitative economy would continue to operate on its own terms, directly in the "currency" of affective engagement and intensities of creative collaboration, or what Whitehead calls "appetite" and identifies as the motor of "creative advance." Internally there would be no division into units, no individual shares, and no contractual transactions in any traditional sense.

All of this is in continuity with the SenseLab project, which since 2003 has been dedicated to the invention of techniques for fostering new, emergent modes of relation at the intersection of art, philosophy, and activism. Its founder Erin Manning and I described its ethos and some of its techniques in our book *Thought in the Act* (2014). The SenseLab's way of working seeks to avoid reproducing not only hierarchy, but any self-perpetuating governing structure. This entails refusing any formal decision-making procedures, whether vote-based or consensus-based. The idea is activate tendencies agitating at the infra-individual level, in order to bring them to expression in such a way that they play out transindividually, in collective experimentations whose improvisational character prevents what takes place from being attributable to individuals. This generates a kind of surplus-value of life that is irreducibly collective, and entirely event-based: an embodied speculation in emergent modes of relation. From this point of view, the value generated by the proposed Three Ecologies economy would be a kind of event-derivative. Like derivatives, it would run on affectively fueled speculative energies, in a kind of metabolism of the future. Unlike existing derivatives, it would function according to what is basically a gift economy, an economy of abundance, without debt or credit. The "decisions" made along the way will be self-deciding: they come from the way in which the tendencies in play in the event play out among themselves, weighted only by the affective force they effectively mobilize, as directly "measured" by what creative propositions take hold with a collective momentum that carries them to realization.

There isn't the time here to go into all the details. Suffice it to say that what we're attempting to do is to hijack the cutting-edge tools of runaway speculative finance to create what is essentially a post-scarcity anarcho-communist micro-society operating in the pores of the dominant economy, specific to a single DAO serving a particular collective project in a way that frees it from institutional funding, and by doing that from all of the neoliberal strings that are increasingly attached to outside funding, whether it comes from private foundations or government sources. If it works, it could expand to include mutual aid systems to help members of the collective survive in the dominant economy. The need to buy food and pay rent will not be going away soon. The convertibility between the particularist currency of the Three Ecologies Process Seed Bank and national currencies is a complicity with the general capitalist economy – but it is also the condition under which it can contrive a partial but effective freeing from it. The Economic Space Agency is working with a number of other initiatives looking to develop collective economies based on notions of the common rather than private property, again taking advantage of the potentials created by the blockchain. Their aim is to prototype new economic platforms, to be made available on an open-source basis, that can be used as templates by others. Ours is the most radical in terms of its attempt to imagine into being a non-exchange-based, purely qualitative, collectivist economy. We may not succeed. It may prove impossible. But even it does ultimately fail, it has already taken our collective along a germinal line of escape.

KW: You started to explain how the vocabulary you're developing departs from classical Marxist terminology. Could you go back to that point?

BM: Another way that what I have been saying deviates from traditional Marxist concepts is that the notion of surplus-value of flow I talked about toward the beginning of the interview calls into question the labor theory of value, which was long considered the sine non qua of Marxist analysis. Surplus-value of flow is an example of what Deleuze and Guattari term "machinic surplus-value" (even when it isn't generated by machines in the narrow sense; machinic can be taken as a synonym for "processual"; Deleuze and Guattari 1983: 232-237). The old labor theory of value is the idea that all surplus-value production is based on leveraging labor time – basically, the theft of a portion of what is produced, as measured by the difference between workers' labor-time, expressed monetarily as salary, and the capitalist's returns.

Earlier, I talked about how the crowdsourcing and data-mining of people's network-enabled movements generate a "surplus-value of flow" in the form of monetizable information. This is the generation of capital out of information, purely as a function of the flow of information. This occurs with little or no labor input – certainly none commensurate with returns. It is an achievement of the algorithmic. You could also cite style scouting in the urban environment, where capital is extracted from variations in style, from the flow of modes of life signalling their difference in relation to one another. The "work" is performed as part of the collective composition of a form of life. This is not labor, but self-affirming, self-inventing activity that is undertaken for its own experienced value.

The mining and monetization of this activity is labor, but again the yield that is arrived at is not commensurate with the work "invested" in the act of capture. The return is excessive. The exploitation is incommensurate, immeasurable. Automation in general, and in particular automation in the form of network-trawling self-executing algorithms, "leverage" life-forms in a similar manner to the way derivatives leverage debt. The leveraging in the financial markets can be by a factor twenty, and that is not considered high. It can run to hundreds of times the nominal value of the underlying assets.

As Elie Ayache shows (2010), in the world of derivatives, pricing, the measure of value, loses its mooring. It becomes a pure effect of the conjunction of abstract flows, of flows of capital intersecting at an arbitrary point where the event of a transaction occurs, often automatically through the decision of an algorithm. Derivatives are justified as a way of "putting a price on risk." But that assumes that risk is calculable, which is little more than a kind of magical thinking conjuring away the contingency endemic to far-from-equilibrium systems with the wave of an abstract wand (whose name is probability). To believe that risk analysis effectively expresses that complexity is comparable to confusing the thermometer for the weather.

To return to the point I was making, with surplus-value of flow, the differential between input of labor and surplus-value tends toward the exponential. In the case of form-of-life mining, the possibility of quantifying the exploitation is no longer present at all. How do you compare the theft of an expression of a mode-of-life's self-affirming with a quantity of profit? The exploitation is in fact directly qualitative. This is easy to see, for example, when indigenous peoples' cultural signs and sacred symbols become commercialized motifs on outdoor wear (to cite a recent example of the poaching of Inuit motifs by a European clothes manufacturer). The grief over the degradation of an expression of a qualitatively different mode of life that has formerly been purely self-affirming dwarfs the grief of the loss of any income the preyed-upon communities might have made by controlling their so-called "intellectual property."

The Three Ecologies project seeks to hold to that aspect of the logic of derivatives that overspills quantification in the production of surplus-value, but to do so in a way that fosters the invention of forms of life, valued in and for themselves, rather than being predicated on the appropriation of their emergence. Rather than leveraging them toward capitalist ends, they would be enabled to self-leverage, to leaven themselves, toward their own emergent ends.

KW: Intellectual property is perhaps the biggest battleground in the arena of network cultures and in the so called digital society as a whole.

BM: Intellectual property is the form in which social or cultural difference – qualitative relational difference – is monetized. It marks a partial belonging, a non-exclusive inclusion, in the capitalist system of movements that do not flow first and foremost according to capitalism's logic, as governed by the attractor of the capitalist relation: a capture of something that is incorporated into capital while remaining resistant to it, that is taken into it but is never wholly of it; a forced complicity (calling for strategic duplicity). The concerns for "cultural preservation," which translates here into the preservation of minoritarian becomings affirming a surplus-value of collective life, and concerns for protecting intellectual property may occur together. But this does not make them the same thing. They are incomparables. The processual distance between them is immeasurable. They belong to qualitatively different logics. A person or group who holds to both cannot be dismissed as a dupe to capitalism, as unwittingly falling into a contradiction, or as complicit in the way the word is so often used with moralistic overtones.

Rather than falling into a contradiction, what they are doing is straddling a schizz. They are living up to their dividuality. We all do that, must do that. Precisely because "there is no outside of capitalism," said once again in a way that does not mean that we are all simply "in" it. At the same time as exploitation ceases to be meaningfully measurable, complicity does as well. All the more reason to insist on directly qualitative understandings of economic processes, on the need for purely qualitative notions of value, and a complex appreciation of how they are articulated to the mechanisms of quantification that are everywhere in capitalism. That is not a simple task. Our understanding of nonquantitative surplus-values of life cannot simply be conceived. As their name implies, they must be lived. Their living beyond capitalism is still to be invented. And all the more reason not to be seduced by the breeziness of the accelerationist thesis.

KW: Today the notion of flow and the notion of real-time flow have become commonplace. The rise of digitality, for instance, hinges upon this idea to the degree that people believe in instantaneous online communication without ever understanding that the movement of data never works without interruptions. Ideally, there is just-in-time delivery of data, but never real-time transmission. However the illusion is uncontested. Moreover it seems to be attributed to any type of movement today (the movement of underclass migrants being an exception). Is this illusion a symptom of the general misrecognition of how infrastructure for movement is actually built and how power permeates it?

BM: This is another prong of the question of quantification, and the difficulty of approaching current cultural and political issues without a thorough calling into question of the tendency to give quantitative notions the last word. The notion of real-time is a chronological notion. It refers to the speed of a transmission through space, increasing in measure toward the ideal point where the thickness of space is overcome, where the drag and delay it represents disappears. This overcoming of space is a fiction. There is no such thing as simultaneity. The idea of attaining it treats space and time as though they could be separated out as independent variables. But there is not a spatial frame on the one hand, and a time-line on the other. Time and space always come together. They come integrally, as a block. There are only space-times – durations. The world is made of duration. Divide an occurrence as far as you can, and what you get is only smaller and smaller patches of space-time, little smudges of duration.

What real-time refers to is really the point at which the delay in transmission becomes negligible, where it ceases to be a noticeable factor. This is a relational reality, having to do with how different durations meet, across differences in scale. Real-time is when the duration of transmission becomes negligible in relation to durations on the scale of human perception – which are themselves relational realities bound up with the larger culturally inflected movements of changing expectations, habits of attention, and perceptual orientations. Real-time is a fiction, but at the same time it is a practical reality. There is always a selling point at which a technology can claim to operate with a delay that is as good as real-time for that particular cultural conjuncture. Real-time is really just-in-time.

You are right to point out that the fiction conveniently glosses over the hard reality of infrastructure and the economic and political power relations that are concretized in it. From the process-oriented perspective I try to work within, the purported overcoming of space can be thought about in terms of deterritorialization. The push toward real-time does enable the flow of images and information to accelerate and circulate farther, faster, through more meanderings, to the point that the force of its anchoring in its space of departure, the trace of its element of spacing, becomes attenuated. As you say, this rebounds on perceptions of the movements of objects and people whose durations are very different to the speed of circulation. The duration of an image's appearance in and passage through the media networks takes the fore, so that it appears as if things, like flows of refugees, have appeared in "real-time" out of nowhere. This has tremendous affective effects. Everything comes as a shock, creating a perpetual state of agitation, of activation, that easily tips over into fear. More and more images begin to prime for fear. It is an odd fact of the affective constitution of human perception – at least present-day networked human perception – that words and images that prime for fear produce nonconscious associations with death.

Studies of priming in experimental psychology suggest that with every perceived threat there appears the horizon of death. Every threat comes with a tinge of existential threat. Certain political movements regularly capitalize on this tendency by mobilizing fear in relation to perceived threats associated with out-groups, treating them as existential threats regardless of their true proportions (or even whether they need to be treated as threats at all). Examples are too numerous to list, from the rhetoric of the right around the Brexit campaign to Donald Trump's wall against Mexico.

KW: Is thinking about infrastructure one way to start bringing the complexity that this tendency elides back into the picture?

BM: Philosophically, it points to the fact that the condition of possibility for every movement of deterritorialization is a reterritorialization. The deterritorialization has been enabled by the painstaking construction of an extensive apparatus for the facilitation of flows whose putting in place has required economic and political will and resources, and therefore stands as an expression of power. Every reterritorialization-deterritorialization constitutes its own space-time of power. Each such space-time is quantitatively as well as qualitatively different. But they conjoin across their difference. Differential flows of commodity goods, flows of human bodies, flows of networked images and information, conjoin in different manners to different effect, depending. The political question is how to act upon that "depending": how, relationally, to modulate the conjunctions.

This is a much larger question than debunking "illusions" or communicating a correct analysis of the complexity of the situation, because there is always that affective element. Affective modulation must be met with affective modulation. Reason, as Hume argued, gives none: alone, it is impotent to motivate action. It cannot give a reason for itself. There is no a priori reason why being reasonable is "better" – unless it is felt to be. The force of reason is found in affect. In addition to giving all the reasons why, for example, the fear of immigrants is unreasonable, the fear of the stranger must be fought on the same affective register as it is produced, but in a different tonality. A politics of care must be made as compelling as the appearance of existential threat. Transindividual sympathy – sympathy operating in radical affective proximity-at-a-distance, across lines of identity – must be mobilized, not as a personal act, not as a moral act, but as a directly political, that is to say, transindividual, act. The shock-effect, the immediation-effect, of "real-time" processing and the agitation/activation it produces could provide as fertile ground for this alternative politics as it does for right-wing politics, if only it is attuned to a different affective tonality, within a different horizon than that of existential threat – namely, the horizon of intensities of life that arise through the collective interplay of differences.

Debunking the fictions, unveiling the illusions, will do little by themselves. That can actually be counterproductive, if it leads to a misapprehension of the affective environment and the counter-powers that may be found in it in germ. An overreliance on critique is destructive of potential, because it perpetuates the myth of reason's motivating power and encourages an underappreciation of the power of affect, where activated potential dwells. Critique is demobilizing. Affect is by nature mobilizing – which is why it can be both dangerous and empowering. The quality of the movements that are primed out of it are what is crucial. What tendencies are tweaked from it are what is decisive.

KW: What do you mean?

BM: Well, if anyone has doubts about the limits of political reason, they need only read an account of a Trump campaign rally or listen to a Trump speech. We were warned. From Ronald Reagan's "facts are stupid things" to the George W. Bush administration's condescending dismissal of the "reality-based community," the role of critical factual analysis and political reason has been on the wane. Trump sounds the death-knell of its power to be determining. Trump can contradict himself from one sentence to the next. He can change his policies today, and change them back tomorrow. His supporters know very well he is doing it. But it does not matter. The Trump-effect is operating in a totally different register, a different kind of "knowing" immune to the need for argumentative consistency. With Trump, a threshold has been passed. I seriously doubt, now that he has won the presidency, that there is any going back.

This is a very complex moment, having everything to do with the politicization of personality. But I am convinced that the extreme personalization of politics we see with Trump cannot be understood in traditional psychological or psychoanalytic terms, in particular in terms of identification. Franco "Bifo" Berardi's recent work, for example, makes the mistake of psychologizing the field of capitalist life. But the dividualization of the person has gone too far for that. We need new tools to understand the profundity of Trump's superficiality, and the force of its reinvention of fascism for the neoliberal age, adapted to the figure of the enterprise-subject and appreciative of the duplicities of the dividual. We need to think hard about the stupidity, the willful stupidity, and the way Trump's personal embodiment of it collectively mobilizes. We do not have a model for this. It is too dangerous to rely on models from the past.

KW: Trying to grasp the significance of movement today one could also talk about the illusion of movement in general: from semi-automatized expressions of infatuation on Facebook to activists who fight and fight without ever sensing that their actions have actually some impact on society. Are we seeing in our time a particular influx of such illusions or delusions? And if so, do they have an effect on the politics of movement?

BM: I just used the word "illusion" in my last answer, which was an admission that the issue is an important one. But at the same time, I felt the need to put the word in scare quotes to distance myself from it. Then again, I used the word "stupidity" unselfconsciously. I think I owe an explanation.

KW: Indeed.

BM: The reason I distance myself from words like illusion is that it brings up the old image, associated with the mid-twentieth-century critique of fascism, of the "masses" deluded by those who know. The idea is that there are those who know, and oppress, and there are those who know even better, and can liberate. Those who know better can outfox those in the know and provide a beacon of reasoned understanding and rational hope, and the two combined into an effective strategy, to the poor deluded masses. Then there is the cynical version that says that no one knows better, but no one knows better than I that no one knows better, so you might as well forget about your pipe-dreams of direct democracy, stop expecting your sappy occupying to do anything but lead to a few hugs from strangers, and just listen to me. This is the Žižek version. I know that neither of these is the way you meant it.

KW: No. My question was based more on concerns for the way in which the technosocial conditions in which we live produce illusions that it is very difficult for anyone to see their way through.

BM: I have a lot of sympathy with this concern, but prefer not to use the words illusion or delusion because of the traces of those other ways of thinking – the too-earnest way of the militant and the way of the cynic – that they might reawaken. I prefer an analytic of stupidity, but one that recognizes that we are all in the same boat together, that none of us is immune from stupidity, or what Spinoza calls "inadequate ideas," because the error at the root of them is of the warp and woof of perception itself. It's constitutional. It has to do with what Deleuze and Guattari sometimes call "objective illusions," true and necessary illusions. Stupidity is holding obstinately to objective illusions, and allowing one's actions, even one's entire life, to revolve around them. This is not just a personal question, and has nothing to do with lesser intelligence or an inability to be rational. It is an existential posture having to do with how one's life is anchored in the field of bare activity, and what potentials that posture toward the immanent limit allows to express themselves – how a body perceives and channels potential.

An inadequate idea for Spinoza consists in identifying an external object as the linear cause of a pain, a distress, or a wrong. These "sad" affects are always relational in their genesis, since they arise from encounters. Every encounter is an affective complex: a patterning of capacities to affect and to be affected. This is not a dualism, but a relational matrix, because both capacities are found on both sides of the encounter. Peirce makes this point: there is no such thing as passively undergoing a force, because even resistance or friction, even shrinking back, constitutes a capacity to counter-affect: they can modulate the application of force, or its follow up. There is no active-passive dichotomy, only affective fields of intermodulation. It is totally understandable, however, that the pain be plotted to an external object. In fact, it is a necessity of survival. The object is the perceptible sign of what is stirring in the relational field – many of whose dimensions do not appear by nature. Among the many things that are active but do not appear as such are tendencies and habits of counter-affection that self-execute nonconsciously. The object is the visible index of the expanded relational field, including what plies it but does not appear in it. Pinning reactions on the appearance of the object is an indirect way of addressing what does not appear – the tendencies and counter-affections that may express next, and impinge on the life of the body. It is a necessary survival strategy, enabling avoidance, or a choice as to the conditions of an encounter. The object's presence visibly indexes logical *nextness* – what can be anticipated based on past encounters and the regularities they presented.

The tendency to isolate the object and glom onto it as the visible index of what in the relational field exceeds present perception and extends in a future-oriented direction into the imperceptibly felt is, paradoxically, of the very nature of perception. It is of the nature of perception to exceed itself. Perception is constituted by this topological torsion, whereby the relational in-which of a pulse of life, the affective matrix of the effectively lived occasion, the impossibility of assigning passive and active roles as long as the relational complexity of that occasion is being fully felt, is projected outward and undergoes a transformation. The complexity is projected onto an objectified region of the external world. It is important not to understand "projection" to imply that there was a pre-existing interiority, and that something in it is displaced toward a pre-existing outside. I'm using the word in the way Whitehead and Simondon use it, which is a bit of a misnomer because the idea is that the "inside" of perception arises with its relative outside, as a co-effect of the objectification of an external region: they are reciprocals, co-generated (this is the case for all inside/outside structurations or systematizations).

The main point for this discussion is that the objectified region stands out as a limited clarification of the complexity of the relational field, which is presented in it in a restrictive expression, strictly in terms of the world's regularities and their anticipatable results. The region indexes what is pertinent to what might come next, with an emphasis on the body's capacity to act, but only as a function of what it *recognizes*. As Bergson said, perception is the way in which our virtual actions actually present themselves. Whitehead calls this necessary but reductive topological transformation of the relational field of life "transmutation." In both cases, the operation is intimately related to the needs and fragilities of the body. It is a necessary operation for the resolution of problems of need.

For example, isolating certain kinds of objects and glomming onto them as food is the way an animal resolves the relational matrix of hunger in a happy way. There is no other way to succeed in eating than to index the complexity of hunger, in its myriad dimensions, physiological, psychological, ecological, to the recognized simplicity of an ingestible object. There is no way to avoid danger to life and limb than to objectify the threat in a way that allows its direction of its arrival to be tracked and the regularity of its movements to be anticipated.

KW: I doubt that one can objectify threat in this way only, because I believe that this approach is very much consistent with Western culture while it plays out differently in other cultural contexts. In Japan for example the idea of living with threat and with uncertainty in general is fairly developed in culture – be it in martial arts or architecture.

BM: Yes, there are certainly other ways of dealing with threat, counteracting this tendency. If the only option were to act in direct accordance with it we would be stuck in reactive postures, and reactionary politics. The problem with the objectification of threat is that what is good for survival is bad for living in the larger sense: for feeling one's way beyond mere survival to greater relational-affective intensities. The transmutation at the basis of perception is true – for all apparently needful intents and purposes. But is in error to the extent that life potential exceeds need, to the extent that the world affords more in the way of life potential than can be recognized in the name of already-established intents and purposes. The focus on the object as indexical sign of the transformational-relational field occults the full range of the complexity of the affective field, obscuring its harboring of potentials for living otherwise.

KW: In *What Animals Teach Us about Politics* (2014), you argue that survival is not the only drive, or tendency, definitive of animal life.

BM: There are relationally intensifying tendencies that are just as strong. These counter-tendencies have to do with play and inventive improvisation (at least in my neo-Spinozist version, if not in Spinoza himself). It is through play and improvisation that adequate ideas may be arrived at – at the ulterior limit of survival. Not against it, but out the far side of its objectifying movement, in a return of perception to the more integral relational field of feeling from which it separated itself out in the object-form. Adequate ideas, for me, are feelings of potential. Since potential is their "object" and potential has as yet no particular actual shape, they are by nature abstract in a way that is not objectifiable in perception.

Perception is a form of lived abstraction, to the extent that it indexes nextness: what is not present, but may be expected to come. But adequate ideas are yet more abstract, in a way that is directly, bodily felt, immanent to perception, and felt as an opening for acting *otherwise,* resonant with the full complexity of the relational field. They are a mode of lived abstraction that I call "thinking-feeling." Thinking-feeling occurs immanently to perception, flush with bare activity. This is the realm of Bergson's intuition and Peirce's abduction.

This brings us to the idea of objective illusion. The objective illusion in what I've just described is treating the object as the efficient cause of the pain, danger, or worry: as a simple, isolatable cause in a linear, one-to-one connection to a sad result. The cause, however, in its fullness, is relational. It is the playing out of the relational field itself, in its integrality. The causation is not fully externalizable. In its fullness, it is immanent to the *event* of the field's integral playing out. It cannot be simply located on the "outside," because the potentials for acting otherwise that the field harbors cannot be exhaustively projected. Their full spectrum cannot be perceived on the outside. They can only be lived-out, immanently.

Stupidity is when the objectified attribution of external causality, which is necessary but also necessarily incomplete, becomes a node around which an entire mode of life is organized. Pain anticipated becomes a generalized posture of fear. The posture of fear is itself felt as a second-order pain, leading to over-vigilance and resentment. This in turn can lead to an overgeneralized reaction that, at the extreme, can extend to hatred of the entire class of objects with which the pain is identified. The merest hint of a threat that can be in any way associated with that class of object becomes a trigger. Soon, the mere presence of an object belonging to the feared class itself becomes experienced as a threat, in the absence of any actual threat. The fear becomes self-driving. Apply this to different classes of people, and you have the kind of racism and Islamophobia we see today.

KW: In today's multifaceted, ubiquitous "threat environment," as military and security experts like to call it, this means that virtually everything becomes a trigger.

BM: Precisely. Signs of threat are everywhere, arriving as out of nowhere at the "real-time" speed of the networked media. The reactive response to this always overreaches its target, because what is being reacted to are generalized signs of the object's class or category, irrespective of individual characteristics or the singularity of situations. The response is always too "big," too generalized, not nuanced enough – basically off-base. Again, this is not a personal error, and has nothing to do with stupidity in the usual sense of a lack of intelligence. It is a processual error, bearing on the way in which bodies are postured into the relational field, and what manner of potential they selectively channel from it as a result. This channels potential limitatively, selecting for *reactions* to threat.

Reaction is a sundering of the affective field. It does violence to it by imposing an opposition between activity and passivity. To react is to assume a posture of passivity in the face of a threat which, for a shocking moment, seems to monopolize all potential for action, leaving a body in suspense, in pained anticipation, cowering before potential rather than embodying a share of it. Reactivity separates a body from what it can do, as Deleuze puts it.

The objective illusion is ultimately that potential can be sundered from the body, that a body can be separated from what it can do. But reactivity does just that: it enacts the illusion. It does the impossible: curtail life's tendency to affirm and expand its powers to be, which are one with its powers to act (which move its becoming). As an aside, Agamben's concept of bare life, with its evocation of the abject body relegated to absolute impotence, is complicit with this operation. An account of the political as founded on bare life stages a becoming-reactive of the very grounds of political thought, suspending the political in the separating of a body from what it can do affirmatively.

The becoming-reactive of thinking-feeling is what Nietzsche rebelled against as the life of *ressentiment*. Ressentiment takes many other forms. All, in one way or another, involve what Deleuze called *a refusal of the event* as a consequence of how the objective illusion constitutive of perception plays out: a simplifying, generalizing, self-stereotyping response to the transformational-relational field that misperceives its potentials, and in doing so curtails them. Although my focus is on right-wing versions of ressentiment, because I find them so dangerous and so off-base, it is important to acknowledge that there are leftist versions of it as well.

My use of the word "trigger" will immediately evoke associations with the vocabulary of the current revival of "progressive" identity politics in North America, which in certain forms assumes *ressentiment* as a political tool of resistance against the opposing identity politics of the right with its resurgent racism: a counter-becoming-reactive. This is certainly understandable and, given the situation, may well be strategically necessary, at least at certain levels or certain moments. But it is important not to forget that it builds from what, from the point of view of a processual take on the subjective becomings stirring in the transformational-relational field, must still be considered inadequate ideas. Serious efforts are made to overcome the inadequacy through attention to the systemic nature of racism and other forms of category-based oppression, which resituates the perceptual triggers in a larger perspective of what organizes patterns of perception without itself being perceptible as such. This steers this form of politics away from "stupidity" as I've been talking about it, as the blank refusal of the event (something the right specializes, even revels in). So does the active reconnection to bodily potentials for resistance achieved through a political use of anger as a reaction. But the starting point is still reaction. And the activation achieved remains wed to an episodically renewed becoming-reactive, which continues to serve as its motor. The political activation paradoxically builds upon the point at which a body is separated from what it can do. Capacitation is arrived at, but its reaccess is always via a detour through reaction, raised to a higher power by negative critique. This formats the achieved capacitation along pre-laid ideological lines. The operation activates, but only to the extent that it is possible to do so by mobilizing anger, the most active of the "sad" affects. But like all sad affects, anger remains on the reactive spectrum. What has been achieved is a becoming-active *of* the reactive (re-activity). Each renewed act of resistance must run back through, from hurt to anger to critique, in a cyclic return to reactive origins. The positive solidarities that are built out of the process are hard-pressed to shake free from their reactive origins, whose mark they bear in the form of a will to judgment accompanied by a hardening of boundaries toward what is judged. Once re-active judgment is unleashed, it, like fear, over-generalizes. Every tendency wants nothing more than its own prolongation and intensification – Spinoza calls this *conatus*. It can happen, following the momentum of the conatus of judgment, that one begins to turn it against one's own and one's allies as severely as one's adversaries. The solidarity created by political anger then devolves into painful divisions among those whom it was meant to unify. The shaming and call-out culture of the left in the United States today is at that cusp.

The point for me is to resituate the systemic context in process, as I defined it earlier. If identity-based practices are strategically necessary at certain political junctures, then it is also necessary to take them to the immanent limit, to supplement them with agitations, with just-emergent activity at the threshold of the knowable, felt unrecognizably, but in a way that is already becoming actionable, without cycling through the detour of a becoming-reactive: with direct plumbings of liminal potential for the integral modulation of the relational field. With accessions to counter-ontopower on an affirmative note, in the key of invention. I understand Fred Moten and Stefano Harney's concept of "black study" in these terms (Moten and Harney 2013).

KW: How does this critique of identity-based politics relate to the concept of the dividual?

BM: In his *Late Notebooks*, Nietzsche gives an account of this becoming-reactive as a constitutive function of perception in ways that relate directly to the concept of the dividual I have been talking about (2003: 34-35, 37-38). He describes what I call bare activity, the transformational-relational field of affect at the level of emergence, where events and actions are just edging into determinate existence. He talks about how conscious thought and voluntary action begin in a nonconscious or liminally conscious welling of bodily sensations, feelings of all kinds: desires, aversions, and germinating abstractions that are not yet owned by an "I" but agitate on their own, for themselves.

None of the elements agitating in this infra-individual "crowd" of forming experience can be unambiguously categorized, he says, as falling on the side of willing or thinking. They are integrally both. In other words, they are tendencies (even the most bodily, apparently purely physiological, among them). Tendencies are of the nature of thinking because what they tend toward is not sensibly present. They are equally of the nature of willing because they are preferentially oriented and are self-executing. Nietzsche underlines their durational nature. Each enfolds, from its particular angle, a feeling of the process under way: a feeling, he says, of the state to leave, the state to be reached, the feeling of this leaving-and-reaching itself, all bundled with many other things, notably the feeling of the muscles tensing for a coming movement, a feeling of the quality of the movement before it comes: an abstract feeling of the movement, without the actual movement – but with its affective force. All of this underlines the primacy of movement we were talking about earlier.

Nietzsche maintains that these durational creatures of the infra-individual primal crowd fight it out among themselves, or combine forces, and then as a consequence of this dynamic interrelating, issue in an action accompanied by a conscious perception. The interrelating cannot be limited to an interiority, because the elements in question are highly sensitive to perturbation. Their infra-individual domain is radically open to the outside. The infra-individual is a field of exteriority, in exactly the same way as the capitalist field (in fact, they entirely overlap, in partial belonging to one another, or in differential mutual inclusion, as I like to put it). The issuing into perception creates the objective illusion that, in Nietzsche's words, there are external multiplicities separable from the crowd, and that among them is to be found a culprit that can be singled out as the cause of any given unpleasant perturbation – and in a sense, all of them are unpleasant, because perturbation is agitating, and agitation is restiveness and discomfiture. All perception resolves the unrest of an agitation on the level of bare activity. Because of this, it is necessary to call radically into question the "hedonic" categories of pleasure and pain, in favor of notions of intensity of activation and the fullness of that activation with potentials.

The moral category of culprit, of a guilty party, is for Nietzsche more fundamental than the category of efficient cause, which is a generalizing abstraction that works to neutralize the odor of moral judgment that comes with ressentiment. With the perception of the guilty party, or more generally the object, an "I" posits itself as an opposing unity. The "I" overlooks the crowd from whose collective willing-feeling it arose. The "I" takes credit for the issuing action. It arrogates the formative activity to itself. It puffs itself up with the affective force of the self-executing movements over which it claims possession. It circles the wagons of its arrogance around the feelings it purports to unify, construing them as arising from the depths of an interiority all its own, rather than from the playing out of a relational-transformational field of unbounded exteriority. Identity is built on this necessary error, incumbent in the genesis of perception. "I" is constitutively stupid.

KW: Could you explain more about the idea of objective illusion or necessary, constitutive error? Which role does it play in your philosophy of perception?

BM: It is easy to grasp using one of Whitehead's favorite examples. We sometimes look into a mirror and mistake what is reflected from behind us as being laid out in front of us. This illusion is the objective result of the conditions of perception. The perception truly expresses the misleading conditions. Objective illusions are truly embedded in the world. It is just that they do not always truly embody the consequences of the actions that might be carried out as a result. If we reach our hand forward, we will not touch the objects in the mirror. When our reach is frustrated, we immediately adjust our perception. This at the same time readjusts the field of the muscular movements that are poised to come, already tendentially present in activated potential (what I call the proprioceptive body-without-an-image). The perception we began with is still there. The illusion, because it is objective, cannot be dispelled. But it can be resituated in a more complex relational field in a way that supplements the perception with an immediate, embodied understanding of the potentials brewing.

This reinstalls us in bare activity, in a way that takes account more fully of the field. We are partially liberated from the perspective of the "I" that arose with the transmutation of the fullness of the causal situation into an erroneous objectification. A fuller field perception becomes available to our body. This field perception contains the original objectified perception as a perspective within it, supplemented by others. Instead of a simply located "I" before a simply located object, cause of our desire or pain, we have a differential mutual inclusion of perspectives, including that of things. In the mirror example, "I" was taken in by the *mirror's* perspective on the world. In one way or another, "I" is always included in a field of relation that is irreducible to its own perspective, that includes it in a larger field brimming with alien, non-I, even nonhuman, perspectives. "We" (our sensitive, thinking-feeling body) are always living larger than ourselves, even if unbeknownst to our "I," and more intensely (more fully potentialized). It is crucial to note that the regaining of the larger field has been achieved, not through any critical reflective consciousness, but through *groping* in error, knocking against the surface of the mirror – *against* the clarity of conscious perception as it presents itself.

So, this is my prescription: relational groping in error, toward a more adequate embodiment of the complexities of the field of life. An embrace of the cyclic, corrective return to bare activity. A noncognitive respect for the crowded affective field. A sympathetic posture of differential mutual inclusion of all of its teaming creatures, however alien their perspectives. A joy in the potential to be regained, snatched from the jaws of objective illusion, even in experiences whose hedonic tone is negative, even in discomfiture. This potential regained is experienced, purely qualitatively, as a surplus-value of life that worth living for itself, purely for the process, purely for the movement and how the movement moves. Follow that as a tendency with conatus, and everything changes.

This "affirmative" stance is frequently mistaken for a "feel-good" attitude with fuzzy new age connotations. It is anything but. This misapprehension, which is currently being widely embraced by "dark" philosophy currents, is based on a fundamental misunderstanding of Spinozist joy, as it is taken up by Deleuze. It cannot be repeated often enough that this idea of joy and sadness is not mappable onto the hedonic distinctions of pleasure-unpleasure, pleasure-pain. Again, this brings us back to the quantitative question. The hedonic distinctions carry an underlying quantitative bias. The attainment of pleasure is understood in terms of satisfaction, and satisfaction is understood as the release of tension. Tension is thought to be physiologically measurable, often in a way that is tied to a biologistic, reductive notion of drives.

This way of thinking is endemic to Freud's thought, and also informs Silvan Tomkins's theory of affect. Joy, understood from the neo-Spinozist perspective, is a question of intensity. Intensity is understood in terms of activation. And activiation is understood not in terms of quantifiable tension, but rather as qualitative potential. For me, this is in turn understood in terms of surplus-value of life. Joy can be tinged with any of the categorical affects, even the "darkest."

In his book on Nietzsche, Deleuze in fact establishes an essential link between joy and tragedy. This is because in when the emergent stirrings of the relational field peak in an event, a cut occurs. The tranquility of the "I," based on its habitual anticipations of a certain regularity, is shattered. This is another meaning of the shizz: the "I" is sundered from "within" (from movements to the ulterior limit folding back-under to the immanent limit, in-coming forth). It is cracked open by strikes of potential whose sudden effectuation hit it like fate. A crack opens between the past and the future, cutting across the anticipatable regularities that normally run from one to the other through the thickness of the present. Fate is the present without thickness, pure cut. In it, the "I" confronts the uncontrollably larger-than-I of the field of life erupting: what Peirce, with uncharacteristic evocativeness, called the "strange intruder." The stranger intruder is not another person. Neither is it the mirror-image alter-ego of the "I." Again, in the example, the mirror reflected an embedded perspective on the *world*. The strange intruder, Peirce says, is the "non-I." The non-I is of another order than the "I." Taken at its widest connotation, it is the event "in person" (representing nothing but itself, meaning nothing but the transformation it brings) with whose complexity "I" must join affective forces in order to live life to fullest potential. Joy is the affirmation of the event, in all its multi-perspectival glory.

This puts it all in somewhat grandiose terms, which might seem to converge with philosophies of the event, like Badiou's, which consider the event to be exceedingly rare, and to constitute a total break with the situation. What I mean is completely different.

KW: Doesn't this hinge upon what you consider to be an event and how you define its political quality?

BM: From my point of view events are always happening. They swarm. The cut of the event is everywhere, all the time, most often in ways that it is possible to neglect, because the regularities of life pick up again right away, and retroactively smooth over the interruption. Benjamin Libet's famous experiments show how conscious perception "back-dates" decisions that set in on the nonconscious level of bare activity to make it seem as if the individual "I" had made them, when it wasn't even there. Only its dividuality was. "I" had been momentarily shattered, disappearing into the schizz, falling back into bare activity, for an instantaneous beat in the pulse of life. This means that the breaking-and-entering of the strange intruder is also endemic to perception. It is as constitutional as the tendency for the "I" to emerge, and continually re-emerge to smooth over its eventful blanking out. Perception blinks. Consciousness "flickers," as Whitehead said. Peirce's theory of the strange intruder is a theory of perception, emphasizing perception's overfullness with non-I experience.

This means that the "tragedy" of the event most often takes "minor," relatively neglected forms. What Erin Manning (2016) calls "minor gestures" can pick up on and amplify the otherwise negligible effects of liminal events. The everyday practice of the minor gesture is far more important than the grand gesture of the militant's faithfulness to the "rare" event. One of the problems with grand gestures (and there are many) is that they leave one in wait for the rare event, deactivated. They are a good excuse to do a lot of nothing, other than trumpet one's own ability to recognize the rare event when it comes and be faithful to it in a way that only the rare few can. There is an astounding arrogance to that idea, and a divisiveness that easily leads to violence (clearly seen in the Jacobin overtones of many currents of thought associated with this way of thinking).

If minor events are everywhere we look, then minor gestures can be also. They are always available to amplify the potential that the minor event imperceptibly expresses. Politics then, can be practiced everywhere, all the time, in whatever situations through which we live our lives, at school, at work, among friends and lovers, in the streets of the city. This is the idea of "micropolitics." For me, the concept of micropolitics is closely akin to the anarchist insistence that the politics practiced in the present should prefigure the relational field to come: that the job of political activism is to make the futurity *in the present* already actionable.

KW: Could you explain your take on micropolitics?

BM: There are two warnings I always feel I have to emphasize every time I bring up the notion of micropolitics.

1) "Micro-" or "minor" are not necessarily synonymous with "small." Again, it is all about qualitative distinctions. "Small" is relative to scale. A minor event in a group interaction is "larger" than a minor event in an individual's perceptual constitution, and a minor event in the media is "larger" than both. The criterion is qualitative. It bears on the smooth-over-ability of the event. Its negligibility. A minor event is imperceptible, but on the verge of becoming-perceptible. It is on the edge of perception's forming, on its fateful, cutting edge. A minor gesture leavens the minor event into perceptibility, so that it is no longer negligible but comes to matter. It is equal to fate. Micropolitics is the politics of making-matter. It is not just any making-matter, but one oriented toward joy. Joy involves the "tragic" affirmation of the integrity of the tendencies plying the relational field, in the name of surplus-value of life. In political terms, this means the mutual differential inclusion of individuals in the event – but

as grasped from the angle of their dividuality, from the angle of their activated, agitating, potentializing participation in transformational-relational field of bare activity. Micropolitics is the modulation of this dynamic differential mutual inclusion, tending toward greater field-intensities.

What I mean by that is a maximally inclusive co-patterning of contrasting tendencies, co-habiting the field in a way that facilitates each fully realizing itself. What I mean by *that* is following the field's tendential bent to its ulterior limit – where it bends back to the immanent limit, where it risks becoming eventfully, irredeemably other, as a function of its own self-accomplishment. The challenge of the co-patterning is to facilitate this passage to the limit of tendencies' intensive becoming in way that they do not oppose and curtail each other.

This requires the processual concern and sympathy I spoke of earlier. That this is practiced in the horizon of becoming-other, rather than in the name of identity, in defense of the self-same, makes all the difference. It potentially erases the paranoia of the other that makes co-patterning impossible. It enables a becoming-active of everybody, against the separative becomings-reactive we all know too well. If this sounds utopic, it isn't. It is just always-as-yet unknowable (but already coming to be actionable, wherever a minor gesture cares to go). It is important to note that the co-patterning at issue is aesthetic. It is at the core of Whitehead's theory of beauty. Beauty, for Whitehead, is not reducible to harmony. It requires an affirmation of discord, a co-operation of incommensurable movements each affirming itself, but in resonance with others.

2) Micropolitics cannot be separated from macropolitics. It is not the not opposite of macropolitics, but rather their underside: associated with what Moten and Harney call the "undercommons." An action always straddles both levels, even if it is oblivious to its participation in the minor. All acts are

duplicitous, participating in both dimensions at the same time, but not with the same effects. It's a kind of aparallel, double-inscription, on correlated but divergent tracks. A corollary of this is that micropolitics, while necessary, is not self-sufficient. Minor gestures always have to play the major, subverting, perverting, hijacking, or hacking it. And however dismissive I can be about the grand gestures of macropolitics, they, like the ressentiment of anti-racist identity-based politics, are strategically necessary at certain junctures.

Under certain conditions – and these conditions are rare – a grand gesture may open the relational field in a way that the minor gestures swarming in it have room to amplify and bloom. It can only do this if it is not stuck in its own programmatic groove: if its programmatic pronouncements carry an illocutionary force, not expressed in their semantic context, that makes them performative of a schizz leaving a proliferating pattern of cracks for bare activity to seep through, each crack oozing potentials for surplus-value of life. The micro-cracks may proliferate to the extent that they converge into a macro-shatter: a revolutionary passing of a threshold.

This illocutionary force of a programmatic utterance is what Deleuze and Guattari call the "order-word" (1987: 75-110). A recent example that stands out is the Occupy Wall Street order-word of the "one percent." It was centrally issued by Adbusters but, against all expectations, opened onto the assembly-form of attempted direct democracy and its swarm of expressive agitations, with just as unexpected powers of contagion. What is needed is an ecology of qualitatively different, but correlated, agitations operating in both dimensions at once, micro- and macro, playing minor gestures and order-words, in alternation and concertation.

KW: You have been using some of the same vocabulary to describe counter-ontopower as you do to talk about the ontopower it opposes. For example potential, and the idea of making the future actionable in the present. One of the ways you talk about ontopower accessing the future in the present is through the notion of double-conditional, the "could have .. would have." How does that work, and how is it different from how counter-ontopowers work with futurity?

BM: That really goes to the crux of why I started working on the concept of ontopower, in the aftermath of 9/11. It seemed to me that the kind of vocabulary that had been used by the revolutionary left since May '68 could just as easily be applied to the dominant regime of power that I felt was consolidating itself in the post 9/11 period, and was already prominent in the management and business strategy vocabulary of the hypercapitalists of the 1990s. But part of me felt that even within this convergence, there was a qualitative distinction to be made, between ontopower as the new dominant and counter-ontopowers. It is the way in which the future is made actionable in the present, the mode of potentialization, that makes the difference. When I use the phrase counter-ontopower, I don't mean that they are the opposite of ontopower, but rather that there are ontopowers that run counter to the dominant mode.

The dominant mode of ontopower crystallizes as a military move. I am referring to preemption. That is the idea that I talk about in *Ontopower* that threat has become so ubiquitous and unpredictable that it is apt to irrupt into a full-fledged danger anywhere, in any form, at any moment. Threat is now by nature "asymmetrical": it is fleeter and suppler than the plodding top-down apparatuses of the traditional military organization and deliberative political decision-making. To wait until a threat materializes into a full-fledged danger is too late: it will already have hit before you know it. So you have to hit it *before it emerges*. This is how George W. Bush put it in his administration's official military strategy.

This makes preemption a directly temporal mode of power. It requires the application of what some military strategists have called "the force to own time." You have to act not *in* time, but *on* time. You have to go back to the "before," as it is in the present. This is the present-futurity of what already potentially brewing, about to brim over into action. You have to act on the incipiency of actions to come. This poses sticky perceptual problems.

KW: Looking at what you develop in *Ontopower* one could ask: How do you perceive what is imperceptibly brewing and may be coming, before it has taken on the contours of a recognizable object?

BM: Well, the only way to do that is to stir the mix, and make what may come, come. Flush it out into taking a determinate form you can determinedly attack. Make it start to "go kinetic" so you can meet it, counter-kinetically, as it is just arising, before it has actioned-out, before it can detonate, and before it can defend itself. This is what I call the "perception attack." The practice of war recenters on the problem of the preemptive perception attack. The perception attack is a way of taking the battlefield into the field of emergence, of weaponizing potential. It is military power becoming-immanent to life's field of emergence: "endocolonizing" (Virilio) the transformational-relational field; capturing change itself. This is a kind of power that is productive of what it fights: the perception-attack leavens the threat, makes it rise, so it can be seen, recognized, and stamped out, before it solidifies into an objective danger.

The time-signature of preemption leads to a paradox. This is a strange kind of paradox that makes everything done in the name of preemption right and true, even if it was wrong (rather than merely undecidable as to its truth or falseness). This is the paradox of the "could-have/would-have," also explicitly articulated by Bush: it turns out, he opined, that Saddam Hussein did not have weapons of mass destruction; but he could have had them for all we knew; and he is the sort that if could have had them, he would have had them forthwith, and he would have used them without a second thought. Therefore, we were right to invade Iraq. The proof? Iraq did indeed become a breeding ground of terrorism.

KW: Witness ISIS...

BM: Yes, the fact that it was the US decision to preemptively invade that made Iraq a breeding ground for terrorism is treated as if it is beside the point. All it means is that the invasion multiplied the opportunities to fight terrorism. It successfully flushed out more threats. To be successful, preemptive attack has to be iterative, cyclically producing and attacking what it fights. Asymmetrical war is the Long War, with many rounds to go, and we shouldn't shrink from it. By this logic, what was wrong was not Bush's invasion of Iraq, but Obama's unwillingness to follow through to the end in Iraq and Afghanistan and to up the ante by invading Syria. His preemptive strategy went drone-ward instead: toward the preemptive war equivalent of the minor gesture (all but imperceptible on the systemic level, liminally war-waging, leveraging surplus-values of the flow of surveillance information). In that direction, he was most willing and eager, becoming the kill-list president.

This logic allows any decision to be factually wrong, but preemptively right, in the perpetual future-perfect tense: when we act preemptively, we *always will have been* right. Faced with any threat, you can say "could-have/would have," will have been.

A threat is different from a danger. It is effectively menacing the moment it is felt as a threat, even if it isn't effectively present. Threat does make itself present, but not in the form of a clear-and-present danger, rather in the form of fear. Fear is the presence of the futurity of threat. Threat, as it presents itself, is a creature of affect. "Reality-based" deliberation has to yield to the affective facts, and the affective facts always indicate preemptive action – if we are to feel secure. Preemption is entirely bound up with security. Wherever security mechanisms are taken, the logic of preemption is in some way activated. So while preemption crystallized in its baldest, most extreme form as a mode of military power, it has proliferated piggy-backed on security concerns. It is also a policing logic on the domestic front. And it is a financial logic – derivatives as a "securitization" strategy says it all. It has gone viral. *Ontopower* explores the viral logic of preemption, with a focus on its weaponization of the relation between the field of immanence and perception and the dynamics of the affective contagions this produces.

The way all of this comes back to the question of the endocolonization of potential and the possibility of making qualitative distinctions that break the symmetry between dominant power and resistance to it, centers on the tautology of the could-have/would have and its paradoxical power to make wrong into a priori right. The making of wrong into right is an operation of legitimation. Preemptive power operationalizes threat in a way that is self-legitimizing, independent of rational argument. As a result, it can be used to legitimate the people and collective apparatuses that wield it by purely affective means.

KW: Do counter-ontopowers, for their part, care about self-legitimation?

BM: No. They are concerned with self-valorization. They don't try to be right when they're wrong, they try to supplement the necessity of error. They also target perception at the constitutive level at which it is just forming, but they do so in a way oriented toward resituating the constitutional error of experience in an expanded field where it takes on qualitative "added-value" as a relational surplus-value of life that makes the event worth living for its own intensity – where, instead of being right, it becomes beautiful. They also operate in an affective register. Counter-ontopower's affective orientation toward the generation of alter-surplus-values it by nature anti-capitalist and anti-militaristic. Dominant ontopower power leverages threat in a way that feeds the capitalist machinery with which the military apparatus is in symbiosis. It also produces a surplus-value of perception, in the form of a productively preempted threat.

However, that surplus-value of perception is not produced for itself, but for the service its playing-out provides for the furtherance of the capitalist process. Preemption's capture of change is captured for capital. It could-have/would have forms a closed loop, channeling the futurity of potential back into capitalist channels. Preemption preempts the openness of the future to the great outside of potential, pre-formatting it for capture by the capitalist process. It makes the future actionable only in order to close it back down, to recapture it in the capitalist relation and the limits of the process it governs.

Counter-ontopowers' affirmation of values other than capitalist surplus-value puts them at loggerheads with the capitalist process, in consonance with non-capitalist modes of relation ungoverned by the logic of capital. As these movements self-affirm, and push toward their mode of relation's ulterior limit, they are in the same movement pushing toward the ulterior limit of capitalism. They must do this in a non-militarisic way, or they will get ugly. When discord plays out in such a way that emergent tendencies oppose and curtail each other, when the tendency of tendencies is to construe their own self-accomplishment as hinging on the annihilation of the others, then the "beauty" of radical differential-mutual-inclusion becomes impossible.

This, unfortunately, is the direction things seem to be heading in today, under the sway of identitarian becomings-reactive butting heads with each other. Counter-ontopower's orientation is aesthetic, not warlike (which is one of the reasons I prefer the vocabulary of activism to that of militantism). Counter-ontopowers move within the horizon of the discordant co-patterning of incommensurable contrasts that constitute Whitehead's beauty. They are tendentially nonviolent, in a way that does not translate into the moralism associated with nonviolence as a transcendent principle. For counter-ontopowers, there are no transcendent principles, just immanent stirrings and self-affirming arcs of self-accomplishment, cycling back in a looping that is cut into, schizzed wide open, by strange intrusions, returning always to the great outside. This is what Whitehead called the "adventure." We should goad each other on to adventure, not beat each other with weaponized potential, or brow-beat each other with militant pronouncements.

2

Movements of Thought

Interview with Brian Massumi
By Adrian Heathfield

Adrian Heathfield: Does movement play a role in your writing practice?

Brian Massumi: Like a lot of people, I have to get up and move. I tend to pace, or do something else that's rhythmic. It's often when I'm in movement and not specifically thinking about what I'm writing that the ideas come. It puts me into the movement of the writing itself. When I was learning to translate, I quickly realized that it's as important, if not more important, to analyze the rhythm of the language. The semantic aspects aren't separate from the rhythm, and other non-semantic factors. I started thinking in terms of managing the paces and pulses of ideas, and the fields of ambiguity surrounding the concepts. Not all ambiguities are equal. Each phrase is surrounded by a field of ambiguity carrying sets of connotations, some broader, others more narrow, some readily accessible, others backgrounded. How they all come together, and the tensions between them, inflects the reading. If you just translate what's there, you miss the inflection, you miss the movement. To translate "faithfully," as if there were a one-to-one correspondence between words in different languages, is just a rigorous way of falsifying. It's the bane of academic translating. There isn't even a one-to-one correspondence between the words that are there in one language and the textual movement of meaning production. Meaning is always fielded.

When I started developing my own writing practice, this lesson stayed with me. I was very influenced by that exercise of ventriloquizing other people's style through translation. I started to pay a lot of attention to the movement of my own writing. There's a point when I'm composing where the movement starts to take over and I begin to feel that instead of me thinking the concepts, the movement is thinking them through me. The concepts are fielding themselves, step by step, pulse by pulse. There's a certain sense of abandon, or perhaps surrender. But it's a surrender to the intensity of a movement of thought in the making, with all its precision – which in the way I mean it includes the way the text manages its ambiguities and distributes inflections. It became very intuitive to me, the notion that thought is a force that moves through personal enunciation, rather than being contained in it.

AH: That's super interesting to me because it obviously connects to a recurring gesture in the rich history of creative writing practices: a giving over of oneself to other forces. I'm thinking about automatic writing, for example, but here it's not so much that you are giving yourself over to the unconscious, but to the non-conscious. Through attention to rhythm, an experience of temporality is opened and present to the process of writing.

BM: Yes, the writing has its own rhythm. Sometimes there are smooth runs with a sense of continuous movement. Other times the writing ties itself up in knots and becomes involuted, sometimes so tightly that I can't necessarily parse it out myself. But I can't take the involutions out, because the knotting's productive. The involution feeds the problem forward. I have to go through the knotting in order to find the next continuing thread in the conceptual weave. This idea of the thinking running itself through me connects with Deleuze's notion of philosophy as being a creative practice in its own right. Philosophy's not about critiquing concepts, and it's not about judging other ways of thinking or other modes of practice. It's about creating new concepts, producing new conceptual movements. This involves a great deal of solitary activity. Because of that, the process can turn in on itself and flounder in a black hole. When that happens, the philosophizing has to find ways of reconnecting to its own outside. That's why Deleuze so often talks about the importance of the non-philosophical field for philosophy. The relation to non-philosophical fields of activity is a way for philosophy to recharge its intensity, to refuel its movement by finding new contributing conditions for the next run and the next pulsing. That involves participating in other forms of activity that are creative, or experimental, or exploratory, and trying to contrive a symbiotic relationship between writing and participatory forays into a non-philosophical field, especially arenas of activity where nonverbal activity is a major factor and the thinking is in the doing or the making – dance, architecture, performance ... Philosophy can and should do field work, bringing the thinking that is in the doing into language, to give it new expression, and in the process renew itself. Philosophy should never erect itself as the judge of correctness or good sense. And it should never 'apply' concepts. It should lift them, in the sense of pirating them or hijacking them, always in seed form, to see how else they might grow; but also in the sense of making them rise, like a leavening.

AH: You mentioned philosophy's relation to non-philosophy, and I was immediately surprised that one can think of forms of thought or action that could be deemed purely non-philosophical. Tracking back to the question of your relation to philosophy itself, within a broader context of knowledge production, one of the things that your writing practice is doing is opening new facings, or encounters with other fields of knowledge making: the sciences, the social sciences, cultural studies, the arts. This is partly about de-hierarchizing the relation between philosophy and these fields, given their historical formations, but it is also about making philosophy more connective, more felt, and more "grounded," in both its pragmatic and ecological sense. You challenge long-installed distinctions in intellectual life: between the empirical and the speculative, common sense and experimentation, "hard" and "soft" thinking, as it were. So I'm wondering do you have a field statement in relation to philosophy itself? What of philosophy needs to be disowned, and what affirmed?

BM: I think philosophy has to continually renegotiate its relationship to other disciplines. I wouldn't say that I'm opposed to disciplinarity, but I am opposed to the control disciplines try to exert over forms of thought that operate otherwise or elsewhere, in the interstices or on the periphery. At the same time, I don't see philosophy as interdisciplinary, in the way it's usually practiced. I think you have to approach any mode of thought or experience as a function of its limits. If you think of a certain kind of activity as oriented by a tendency, you can ask where that tendency leads when it is taken to the limit. That amounts to asking what that mode of activity can do when it's doing what it does best, and in what sense that is something *only* it can do. Take it on a run to the limit of what it can do, and see what comes, as an experiment. Philosophy is the activity of running thought experiments.

In the first instance, this way of doing things separates a mode of activity from others. When philosophy runs away with itself, takes itself to its own limit, and truly creates concepts, one thing that is guaranteed to happen is that its thinking will outrun utility. It will be tapping experimentally into the futurity in the present, it will be bringing to expression powers of thought that are just dawning. The context is not quite ready for them. They lack a proper context. The concepts will be breaking new territory, and function and utility will have to catch up, new ones will have to be invented, for which new contexts will emerge. Intensely coherent uselessneess is a symptom of philosophy's success.

But in a second moment, something else happens. Because right at that moment, of intensest creativity, philosophy falls out of itself, into an absolute proximity with other modes of activity. It's maybe easier to see what I mean using another example, say the senses. What can vision do best, what can it do that no other sense modality can do? I would say, colour. Touch can do form and outline, in its own way, but colour is untouchable. Yet where colour is operating most intensely, say in color field painting, there is suddenly a sense of movement *in* colour. Vision has taken up into itself another sense modality. Kinesthesia, which in its own mode is invisible, has become visible. And at the same time, vision has become kinesthetic. A similar thing happens when philosophy reaches the limit of what it can do. When it brings the futurity in the present to expression, it's verging on the emergence of new contexts. What is that, if not political? Or at least proto-political. Couched in those dawning contexts are new forms of perception, new modes of experience. And what is that, if not aesthetic, or at least proto-aesthetic? If the emphasis, for example, is on new experiences of space, philosophy is absorbed in becoming architectural – at the same time architecture is absorbed in becoming philosophical. It's a two-way transformation, where the culmination of one mode of activity opens out onto another, or others, in a shared state of renewal. The non-philosophical – the political, the aesthetic, everyday modes of experience, other disciplines – reasserts and renews itself at the end of a successful philosophical run. The activity of philosophy starts and ends with the non-philosophical.

The point is that the relation of a mode of activity to others is immanent to its exercise. It's not inter-, its *infra-*. But I'm talking here of modes of activity, not disciplines. It's not necessarily the case that a discipline that claims rights over a mode of activity actually takes it to its limit. More often, it curtails any movement to the limit. Philosophy departments are typically the last place you'll find philosophy practiced creatively in the way I'm talking about. Disciplines are concerned with gate-keeping to safeguard their prerogatives, and with reproducing themselves institutionally. That's why I never formally studied philosophy, and have never taught in a philosophy department. The authors I was interested in were being kept outside the gates, and I had to go into French literature to do philosophy. That interdisciplinary move was a necessary condition for doing philosophy for me. I think the non-philosophical has two senses. The primary sense is philosophy's convergence on other modes of activity from within its own tendency, taken to the limit. You could call that transdisciplinary. Then there's a secondary sense of the non-philosophical that is a consequence of that, which is interdisciplinary moment, when philosophy nests itself, cuckoo–like, in another arena of activity, in order to be able to follow its own movement unencumbered by the discipline that has grown up to contain it. Interdisciplinarily, if it's doing its job, philosophy will never be entirely accepted. I currently teach in a communications department. I'm treated well, and what I do is tolerated, but only as long as it doesn't lead too many students astray or take up too much space. That kind of uneasiness is because of philosophy's necessary relation to the useless, its outrunning of function and utility. Disciplines vie for funding and students by making arguments about how socially useful they are. The first thing I tell my students when I start a new class is that if I'm truly successful in my teaching what I will teach them will have absolutely no immediate benefit for the job market. This doesn't exactly endear me to most of them. They're supposed to be paying for a service, after all. Philosophy is not a service industry.

AH: In your recent writing, the idea of the event has been very important and I take from that the notion that an event is something elementally transformational. It is something singular; something old and new, continuous and discontinuous, at the same time. But it is also extinguished, it evaporates, it disappears. I'm wondering how this notion of event relates to the everyday, and to the mundane even [dog barking] – and there it is! It was a mundane event. Now we don't even need to do the discourse. [laughter] If one thinks in this way one sees, then, event everywhere. But for there to be an event at all doesn't there need to be a bracketing around that event? There would need to be a constitutive zone or condition of the uneventful? Is there then an event of the mundane or even of the banal?

BM: I would say the mundane is full of events. They're just events that on the surface present themselves as being more repetition than variation, or that background themselves behind other events or objects that might stand out in relief. The object is not a non-event. It's just a slower-paced event compared to our activity around it, or toward it. An object is full of activity, in it and all around. There's activity inside it that's invisible to the human eye because it's too small or too fast. The material that composes it is churning with action on the molecular level. And there's activity around that changes it at a rate too slow to see – the way it weathers for example, or goes through a phase-shift, like sap to amber. In our mundane relation to objects, we connect with them between these two extremes, where the object is sluggish relative to the swiftness of our hands, but not too slow to grasp. The object is not the opposite of the event, it's a certain nexus of events. So you're right, if you start rethinking philosophy emphasizing the eventfulness of life, you have to rethink a host of concepts.

You can't start with the object as it's usually thought of, as a more or less inert lump of matter. You can't start from a concept of substance either, because a nexus of events has relation, it's a composition of movements, but there's nothing underlying them, they hold each other in place. Everything is in the way they come together and co-compose. There's no stuff. If you go down far enough, all you reach is the void, the restless energy field of the quantum void. You can't start with the subject either, because a nexus of events is in the world, not in an interiority. There is only one place to start, and that's with *activity*. You have to say that the only thing certain is that there is activity always going on, and that's what the world is made of. And when you say that, you've just added to the activity. Thought itself is an event. So start there, and take it to the limit.

A common misconception about this kind of event- or process-oriented philosophy is that it's a philosophy of pure flow or pure continuity. This is a tenacious misunderstanding of thinkers like Bergson, Whitehead, and Deleuze and Guattari, which has always surprised me. Because you just have to read one page of a book like Deleuze and Guattari's *Anti-Oedipus* to see that they make the cut as primordial as the continuity (1983). In a process, it's not continuity *or* rupture, it's always both. For example when the dog interrupted us, he'd taken a big breath, he'd braced himself for us going by, he was ready for us. Then he let go, and the bark that emerged had an arc to it. It had an internal rhythm, it was pulsed, it was composed of mini-events of variation of tone and loudness. But the mini-events folded into each other to compose *a* bark, with an overall affect: surprise. That affect was also an immediate effect: it gave us pause. It cut into our conversation, it produced a rupture in it. The bark was a single event for our conversation, even though it was composed of any number of mini-events. It figured in our conversation as a continuity: one bark, rolling across its pulses. It presented itself with a dynamic unity of unfolding that cut it off on the one hand from the continuity of the ambient background sound, and on the other made it cut into the continuity of our conversation: cut *and* continuity.

So you have to think in terms of rupture and continuity at the same time, which means putting them together processually. It's a distraction that goes nowhere to talk about them as oppositions or contradictions, because that's not what they are.

They're co-factors in process. They co-occur, and events happen between them. The way that co-occurring plays out will give the event a certain arc, a certain lifetime, depending on how it's conditioned, how it's energized. And then it will dissipate, it will "perish," as Whitehead says. Every event, however mundane, however small, has a singularity to it. There's always something different about how it plays out, there's a unique experiential flavor to it. So when we talk about the "new" from a process philosophy point of view, we're not talking about a new object, or a new thing, or new gadget, or even a new function. We're talking about the singularity of events – how each is a unique coming-about, even if it's also a repetition, even if the "same" event, like taking a step, which has happened a million times before. The new has to do with what Daniel Stern calls "vitality affect." That's the sense of *this* happening *here and now, just this once in just this way* – and then it's gone. It's the registering of the singularity of this event. The new is the event's *eventfulness*. It's the event-quality of the event. It's not a characteristic or property of things.

AH: It's a slightly obvious question but maybe it produces something interesting: that seems to imply then that there may be very little distinction between an aestheticized event and a natural event as such. The aesthetic runs all the way through perceived reality. But for an artist, that might be a difficult thought. There is quite an investment in traditions of art and performance practice, of rupturing forms, by opening to the event, to the occasion. Are there any specific qualities that you would identify with an aesthetic event that you would not identify with a natural one?

BM: I wouldn't make a sharp distinction between them, because if you think about events in the way I was just talking about, every manner of event is pressing, or present in tendency, in the germinal phases of every other event. Every event detaches itself from the background noise of all the events it might have been. Which is a challenge more to history than to art, because it implies that to write history you have to do something like what Foucault calls archeology. It's not just about the causes of what happened. It's as much about the consistency of the might-have-been – the background of potential that events cut away from. It's as much about the doable as the done, and the sayable and the seeable, as the said and the seen. You have to make a distinction between conditioning and causing. The conditions of an event are always much broader than any linear causal relationship. The question of conditioning is: in what way, for this event, in its germination, have other modes of activity come into play, only to fall out of its rising arc? Even so, how may they have resonated together, and with the singularity of this arising event? How may they have interfered with each other, to inflect the event's happening, even though they didn't enter directly into its constitution? Might that tension, that germinal intensity of activity, have contributed to the singularity of what happened as it followed its own tendency to completion? Might it even potentially complicate the birth of the event so that what happens might actually have to take a new tack, even invent a tendency for itself? I would situate the aesthetic on this nascent level of event-conditioning. The aesthetic has to do with the overfullness with potential of what actually happens, and the renewal that comes of it. It's that dimension of experience, and any attunement to it. I wouldn't separate out the aesthetic as a separate domain or realm of activity. The aesthetic is a dimension of every event's arising. The question then becomes a very pragmatic and constructive one. By what means can that dimension of a given event be brought out? By bringing it out, can you develop the aesthetic dimension into a tendency in its own right? What would happen if you did, and then took that tendency to the limit of what it could do? That would be the job of art: to distill the aesthetic dimension belonging to every event into an event in itself.

Going back to the idea of vitality affect, and our discussion of the dog bark, I was saying that you feel it coming even before you can consciously understand what the event is about, in the sense of reflecting about it. At that first exhalation of the dog barking, you're already in the barking before you've consciously identified it as barking, you're in the arrival of the bark, in a way that takes you directly into its movement. You know you're in it, before you can register that fact reflectively. You're already inducted into the event, thinking it on the same level you are feeling it, before you can reflect. You're feeling the singularity of this event, at the same time as your induction into it is awakening all sorts of things that retrospectively, when you have the luxury of reflecting on it, you will recognize as belonging to that *kind* of event. Every barking is singular, but no event ever comes just once. They repeat, and the repetition is just as much a part of what makes the event as its singularity. So at the same as we're feeling the event dawning, we're starting to feel the *likeness* of the event. This isn't a comparison yet, because you can only compare when you have an outside vantage point on more than one event, but here you're absorbed in this event. The likeness of the event is *to itself*, as it's occurring. It's how the event carries its relation to other events, past and potential, in itself, presenting both what makes it comparable to them as one of their kind, and its own singularity that sets it apart. The likeness of the event to itself, in itself, is the difference the event has in its own constitution between what's new in it and what could be recognized in it, or between how it can be experienced as a repetition of a certain kind and why it has to be experienced at the same time as a variation. This is a minimal difference. Later, on reflection, when things are quiet, that minimal difference can be pried open in reflection, making space for comparison with other events.

This likeness of the event to itself is as much a part of the event as what actually happens causally, for example in terms of what molecules shift place. It's directly experienced, even though it can't be equated with the causal movement. It's in the movement of the event as such. It's part of the quality of the event. The qualitative aspect of the event that you can't reduce to quantifiable movements is what I call the semblance of the event (Massumi 2011). My proposition is that this qualitative aspect is where the aesthetic dimension lies. That minimal difference is what the philosopher Raymond Ruyer calls its "aesthetic yield." The question for art is: what can be done with that? What may art do? Does it develop that minimal difference into a big difference that might lead to new reflections? Does it lift that event-quality out of the event, holding it in suspense? Does it suspend the already established functionings of the organism and the already established meanings of the context, at least for an instant before they fall back into place as the event peaks? Does it suspend the connection to form and function, and allow the dawning event's fullness with potential to vibrate? If it does that, where can that lead? What can it bring it out, if anything? Does it short-circuit reflection? Or carry it to a higher power?

AH: The vitality affect of the event, and its relation to history, has been a very big problem for performance art. For such a long time performance was associated with presence, with a presentational force as opposed to a representational order, and so the document, the archive, historiography, etc. were seen as suspect iterations in relation to the force of the event. But that has led a lot of people to say this is really reifying the event; entangling it with "the authentic," putting a lot of pressure and investment into very specific qualities of the event, which may be re-performed in other representational forms. So we move from trying to think about the ontology of performance as absolutely founded in disappearance, towards an ontogenetic model where performance is recurring iteratively, proliferating differences through multiple forms.

BM: Yes. I think that iterative structure, the structure of variation and repetition, has always been part of every art and every craft. Technology has accelerated it. Everything is pre-adapted for iteration, for quick capture, turnover and distribution. But it's not just a distribution of things, it's also of events. If you think of it that way, it raises a whole new set of questions. It makes reification less of a focus. Things don't stand still long enough to become fixed. There's still reification, but it's just a thinner and thinner threshold between turnovers. Which means that the idea of reification as standardizing and homogenizing is out of date. If you do start from activity as the base concept, and move into an event-based approach, it's really all about singularization. Reification is just a passing phase in a process of continuing variation. Contemporary capitalism is more moving than it is reifying. Which is not to say it's better than its earlier incarnations, like the industrial capitalism that the concept of reification was designed to grapple with.

AH: When we encountered the dog earlier, you talked of the phenomena of the dog arriving before they arrived. You gave the dog bark a particular temporal dynamic as a phenomenon. My sense is that this term "semblance" is really important for you in relation to this kind of occurrence. I take it immediately when one says something like "semblance" that it is distinguished from resemblance, and from representation. It is already something that is less than, or even more than that. I also understand from what you are saying that a semblance is something informed by the co-constitution of the senses …

BM: Yes.

AH: … all the senses interrelating in particular ways. A semblance is then a kind of feeling of something, but it's a feeling of something not yet conscious, not yet arrived.

BM: Exactly. It's about the interrelating of the senses, but doesn't correspond in any direct manner to sensory input, however multi-channeled. The lived quality of an event, its vitality affect, which I associated with the semblance, can't be plotted back to any particular sensory input. It doesn't correspond to a particular impingement of light on our retina, or sound on our eardrums. You can't think the event without thinking beyond that level of sense-impression. The semblance of the event is nonsensuous. But that doesn't mean it's an illusion. It's as much a part of the reality of the event as the movement of molecules and photons and their physical impingements on our sensory apparatus. Semblance is a way of saying that there's something else in play that isn't sensuous and in no way resembles it. Does a sound wave impinging on our eardrum resemble a dog? I've never encountered a dog in the shape of a sine wave. Does a photon that hits our retina resemble an object? Photons are by nature invisible. But they give rise to vision. That's the point – the event never resembles its conditions of emergence. It surpasses them, into its own reality as an event, striking on the level on which it is experienced. It can't be reduced to any other level. But at the same time it can't be separated from any of the levels that contribute to its emergence. It wraps them up into its own arising. Some of those enveloped levels are sensuous, in other words correspond to a physical impingement on our body's perceptual apparatus, and some are already nonsensuous. For example, every event wraps its immediate past into its unrolling. Through the immediate past come more distant regions of the past, in the form of various inheritances passing down the line of events as they repeat and vary. The immediate past is no longer. What is no longer has no physically impinging presence, and so can't possibly correspond to any sensuous input. It's by nature nonsensuous. So is the immediate future that the event tends toward, following the momentum it has inherited from the immediate past. All of this is something Whitehead emphasizes, and makes fundamental to his metaphysics (Whitehead 1967: 180-183).

One example of a semblance that I often think about goes back to my childhood. It was just a small event, but it has stayed with me. I was in a car and a van sped past, lost control, and left its lane. It tried to swerve back in the right lane without hitting our car, and it rolled over several times. There's a kind of untimeliness to an event like that. It happens so quickly, in a state of shock, that you're bracing for what's happening without cognizing it. You're *aware* of what's happening, of course, intensely aware of it, but not in any way you would compare to your normal state of reflective cogitation. You know exactly what's happening, but you couldn't put it into words. The understanding comes as a feeling, with a distinct affective tonality and force. But in the feeling there is already a thinking of the event. You're braced for what might come. All kinds of felt hypotheses about what exactly will happen in the end hit you en masse. I call this 'in-bracing,' because it's less that you're in your head bracing for what's coming, than you're in the potential of the event, body and soul, braced into the event as surely as your seat belt braces you to your car. You are utterly absorbed in the event, at no distance from its happening. In that bracing, you can't know exactly how it will turn out, but you certainly know how it's "like" to be in that event. That's pretty much all you know. That minimal difference I was talking about before is intensified, to the point that it feels uncanny. You have a weird sense of déjà-vu, knowing full well that this is a singular event. The déjà-vu is not a comparison to a past event. It's the weird, intensified feeling of this event's likeness to itself: "so this is what it's like be in an accident ..." It's like the event is doubled. At the same time it is intensely itself, it is just as intensely like itself. That déjà-vu feeling is the semblance of the event. It's like the abstract double of the event. What it boils down to is the feeling of the event's potential to be just what it will have come to be, while the potential is still playing out. It's like a feeling of the dynamic form of the event, its arcing out of potential into its own completion. This is a thinking-feeling, in the sense that the immediacy of the feeling isn't separable from abstractness, from the abstractness of potential, and from the semblance as the event's uncanny self-abstraction. None of that can be parsed out into separate sense inputs. The sound of the tires screeching heightens your seeing the swerve. You're not hearing separately from seeing. You're experiencing their interrelationship. The hearing and the seeing wrap up together in the semblance.

Another example I like comes from the philosopher Suzanne Langer. It's the example of being in the kitchen in front of the sink washing dishes when you sense a scurrying in the periphery of your experience. It's a niggling feeling that you couldn't even identify as something you're hearing. Even if it's just a niggling, it braces you into the coming event. You know already it's coming, without knowing what it is that's coming. Then you see a movement on the periphery of your vision. It's not yet a sight. It's a niggling feeling at the edge of vision. The scurrying sound and the scurry of almost-seen movement fuse. In their interrelation, an immediately lived hypothesis imposes itself: mouse. You brace for a mouse event. You are in-braced into a mousing event. The event is immediately vectorized in terms of its mouse potential: the mouse could be coming towards you, it could be going past you, you could be going in one direction, it could be going in another. You 'see' all this as a tangle of abstract lines – mouse trajectories and human trajectories, in their interrelation. Mouse tendencies and human tendencies dancing around each other, playing themselves out together. The tangle sorts itself out as soon as you consciously register the mouse form, as soon as you cognise it. Now the event resolves into one abstract line: the immediate past of the mouse's movement arcing toward a terminus. You don't just see the mouse. What you mainly see is the arcing, its dynamic form – its semblance – and you act accordingly, by jumping aside or rushing after in attack. What you've seen and act according to is the semblance of the event. Nothing sensuous corresponds to it. What you're "seeing" is the abstract double of the event, still with some unresolved potential (the mouse could still veer, you could hesitate between fight and flight). So the semblance weaves together the immediate past, the immediate future in the dynamic unity of the event that is seen without being visible. If you just saw the visible mouse and not the dynamic unity, you'd be powerless to react. The event is moving too fast to visually track the mouse. You don't so much see the mouse, as the abstract mouse-line of the event.

AH: So thinking about the semblance as it arises in the aesthetic, it reminds me a lot of that phrase of Bergson's: "a little nothing that is everything in a work of art." And in relation to aesthetics, because of its base in the interrelation of the senses, I imagine the semblance has a very strong relationship to the invisible, to the untouchable, to the silent. But I'm wondering if it's not previously figured in many ways in art history and aesthetics, and two immediate examples where it might be found would be in the ghostly, and in the sublime, the presentation of the unpresentable. But the semblance seems more promising in relation to both, because it is something that really thinks the imperceptible, not just through sight, but through the senses and phenomena of the whole organism, the whole human animal.

BM: The semblance has an uncanniness, but it doesn't have to be so grand as the sublime or so destabilizing as the ghostly. You could think of the semblance as a kind of ghostliness doubling every sensory experience. The ghostliness is related to the feeling of déjà-vu I was talking about. We experience the abstract line of the mouse event as if it were in vision, when it actually isn't. The semblance always comes out of the interaction between senses. It's what Michel Chion, the cinema theorist, talks about as a synchresis: an emergent effect that works across sense modalities and has a unique quality that neither has alone. (Chion 1994). He gives examples of how we have the experience of seeing things in a film that are actually only heard. But if the timing is right, the sound's interaction with vision creates a sight that was "heard." It's actually a fusion of hearing and vision: audio-vision. It's what happens between the two, in the way they come together. The semblance always happens between two, or between three, or between any number of senses that might be involved. It's not in a sense modality. It's "amodal." What's between two sense modalities is not in one or the other, it's in their relationship, and in that relationship a unique form of experience emerges that has a quality all its own that's amodal. It always has to do with the composition of the senses. That means that you can manipulate or create or construct semblances by how you technically rearrange their conditions of emergence. That little nothing that is everything in art that you were talking about in relation to Bergson, I think that it has to do with the amodal, and the idea that what emerges on the amodal level doesn't resemble its conditions of emergence. That aspect of the event's non-resemblance to its own conditions – which is at the same time its likeness to itself – means that the event is taking a certain distance on itself. That aspect is not often attended to directly, but it can be. It's that little something, or little nothing, that makes all the difference, that effectively makes the event the event that it is, with its unique vitality affect. That's precisely the event's aesthetic dimension. For example, if you have an interactive form of art based on conversation or conviviality, what makes it art, and not just a conversation? A conversation has its own mode of activity. A conversation becomes artistic when the conditions of its occurrence are set in a way that offsets it slightly from its own mode, that create that minimal distance of conversation to itself, giving it a unique vitality affect that just any conversation doesn't have – a little something extra. In what we recognise as an art context, we're primed to attend to the something extra. Art brings the amodal, and the qualitative element of vitality affect that coincides with it, to more palpable expression.

AH: Part of what you're invoking in these phenomena seem to be elements of experience that are in some way or another excessive, unpossessable. But I'm wondering how this relates to aesthetics in the sphere of what people are calling the "experience economy," where what is being traded, bought and sold is no longer simply a material object, but a set of affects associated with objects or an experience itself, or a "service" as one might say, in slightly older language. There has been a vast expansion of experiential practices in contemporary art in the last twenty or thirty years: the development of relational art, then participatory practices, the reincorporation of performance art into the visual arts institutions, and now dance has followed this assimilation. So I'm wondering what you think of experiential art practices in this capitalized context? What happens to those aspects and dynamics of excess, of redundancy or waste, when capital has become so great at turning those very phenomena into value?

BM: That's a very good question. I was talking earlier about how an event-based way of thinking centers on process. Capitalism itself is a process, the prime process of our epoch. As a process, it shares a lot of the characteristics I was talking about. As markets have become saturated with consumer objects, capitalism has become more and more focused on selling experience. Its constant need for turnover means that it's centrally concerned with the emergence of experience, its repetition and variation in new iterations. This focuses it on what I was just describing as the aesthetic dimension. When I was talking about vitality affect and the semblance as a qualitative double that is the thinking-feeling of what's happening, but comes in excess over any literal interpretation of the event, I was talking about a kind of *surplus-value* – a surplus-value of life. Surplus-value of life is in excess over function, utility, already known structures of meaning, and even the strictly material conditions of the event's occurring. It's what art is in the business of producing. But more and more, capitalism is literally in the business of doing the same thing. We all know the slogans: the experience economy, the creative economy, immaterial production. Capitalism, at its leading edge, is mad about producing surplus-values of life. It's excited about inciting movements of emergence and of expression, tendencies and potentials. But what it's most excited about is capturing them – channeling them into the production of its own mode of surplus-value, which is monetary surplus-value. It's all about monetizing experience, to the point that for the neoliberal economy we are no longer human beings, but "human capital." Capitalism has learned to exploit experience at its emergent level, and to channel the emergence toward its own ends, which are purely quantitative: more. More turnover, more profit, always faster. It's all about excess, but not qualitative excess. It's about quantitative excess, which can only be produced capitalistically in a way that mass produces inequality.

The problem that I grapple with is that this emergent level is also where you connect with the aesthetic dimension. That means that when art goes there, in a sense it's going into the heart of the capitalist process. There's almost no way for artistic activity to evade capitalist capture. Just think of the emphasis today on art-based research. The neoliberal university, which is more and more indexed to the market economy, loves it because it sees it as a way of corralling art for the capitalist process, as a way of capturing the surplus-values of life art produces and channeling them into monetary value production. It sees practice-based research as a product development laboratory for the creative economy. There is no getting around this question of complicity. Some people, like Žižek for example, say that it invalidates the whole event-based, process-oriented approach, that the whole approach is complicit through and through because of it. But another way of thinking about it is that it gives creative practice a point of contact with the capitalist process, at that problematic node where it converges with aesthetic activity. Why can't that be a strategic node, where the potentials entering into process might be leveraged in a different way? Perhaps they can be made to evade being captured for the market and channeled toward the production of monetized surplus-value. Perhaps countertendencies might be found at that emergent level that are affirming surplus-values of life as values in themselves, and not just as qualitative means to quantitative ends? Let's face it, we're all complicit with the capitalist process. There's no standing outside it. There's no way of surviving without being complicit with it. So the question for me is less to denounce complicity. That's all too easy. The question is to experiment with modulating complicity, to learn how to inflect it toward other kinds of emergences which, at the limit, might be capable of composing a purely qualitative alter-economy of life-value. I think that imagining and constructing qualitative alter-economies is a major task of our time. And it's a task that can only be done collectively.

AH: Can I ask you about Tino Sehgal in that regard? In many ways Sehgal's work seems to embody that particular tension between the dynamics of capture by capital and some potential movement, or escape velocity out of capital. You performed in Sehgal's *This Situation* recently here in Montreal: a piece that convenes a scene of public discourse on debates in critical thought and philosophy. One of the questions there, in terms of this tension with modes of capture, is around the nature of the convening of a space of public discourse: to what extent that space falls into generic formulae of discursive exchange, and therefore into a sanctioned knowledge economy? Or to what extent it can carry or hold a rather amorphous, constantly evolving, differentiating space of discourse? Does that resonate with your experience of making this work?

BM: Yes, well I think it's a very good example because Sehgal is very consciously playing on modes of complicity. And he's often criticized for bringing relational or participatory art back into the gallery, and for selling the work. But he's selling it in a different form. He forbids documentation, visual or auditory. What he sells is a set of instructions for remaking the event. So he's playing on the immaterial products of the new capitalist order, finding a way to literally sell abstract germs of artistic events. I wouldn't fault him a priori for choosing to work inside the gallery, and I don't think complicity in itself is an adequate critique. The question is, given this choice of emplacement, and the patterns of complicity that come with it, is there something else that can be made to come to pass? Is there something different that is being made to happen that is not reducible to the complicity, but might in fact be enabled by it, and wouldn't come about without it? In addition to producing a monetary surplus-value for himself that allows him to keep his work going, is Sehgal in any sense creating surplus-values of life for the participants and/or for the performers? *This Situation* is one of those artworks that play on the conversational form, as we were talking about earlier. So returning to that discussion, the question for me is, does he make a semblance of it? Does he open the minimal difference of conversation to itself so as to make it an intense likeness of itself, foregrounding the thinking-feeling of what is happening as it happens? And does having the piece in the gallery enhance or dampen that gesture?

In the case of *This Situation*, I think it's actually a very different experience for the participants than for the performers. I can only talk about it from the performers' side, and I have a feeling that it succeeds more on that side. Just to explain briefly what it's about. There's a set of quotations from thinkers starting in the sixteenth century going forward on just the kinds of questions we've been discussing: the relation between the aesthetic and the political, between the aesthetic and the economic, between work and leisure, and on the nature of creativity. There are six performers in the room standing in set position against the walls. Everyone has memorized an assigned number of quotations. A performer pronounces a quotation at a moment of their choosing, introducing it with a stereotyped formula mentioning its date but not its author. Then everyone shifts positions in a predesignated pattern, and once they're in their new positions, there's a discussion coming out of the quote. The positions are tableaux vivants gesturing to famous paintings in the European canon. The interaction is quite ritualized. As they are speaking, the performers are supposed to be gesturing nonstop at an excruciatingly slow pace in a rhythm that doesn't match the rhythm of their speech. There are certain ways for interpellating the public in the gallery, inciting them to speak. The performers are instructed never to comment on the performance, even in response to a direct question about it from the public. Meta-reflection is forbidden. There are ritualized mechanisms for triggering a cut in the discussion and a move to a new position in order to deal with things like that without directly addressing them, just making the performance move past them.

So there is a whole choreography that ritualizes the conversation. I think this drives some people crazy, because they feel it's not a "real" conversation, like it's less than one. But that's the point. The point is to make conversation reflect upon itself, not just to reflect in conversation on other things, and certainly not to reflect *on* conversation. When the performance is working, that little something less becomes a something more. The ritualization does create the conditions for a semblance of a conversation to emerge. The experience doubles over on itself. You're experiencing the semblance of the conversation at the same time as you're experiencing the conversation, and they resonate in each other to yield a peculiar vitality affect. This is not quite like any conversation you've been in before. There's also a very interesting dynamic that sets in over time, as the performance ran for seven hours a day six days a week for two months, with the performers working in shifts. The conversational form begins to exhaust itself. There are a limited number of quotes, which makes for a huge amount of repetition for the performers. After awhile, you start rolling your eyes when a certain quote comes up again, because you've exhausted everything you have to say about it. So then you have to find a way to deal with your own potential boredom. This is actually the point where the performance becomes truly relational, because you can no longer just draw on your own resources – you've already exhausted them. You have to find ways of triggering the other performers into seeing the issue differently, so they say something different, and then you can work from that to generate something to say that you would never have thought of saying otherwise. That's where it begins to get inventive. It becomes truly improvisational. It is no longer you who are speaking, or some other individual. The conversation passes between. It truly becomes a collective enunciation – a subject-group as Guattari would say. It doesn't happen all the time, in fact it's pretty rare that it happens, but for me as a performer when it did happen it reenergized the whole piece. The weird thing is, the whole thing gets most intense at those moments, where you're no longer speaking in your own voice, or performing your individual point of view. You even start saying things you don't actually believe, because the situation seems to be asking for it to be said. It becomes a kind of group thought experience of what is it possible to think with these people, in this situation, around the issues brought up by the quotes. It does become a quite singular situation. It's different each day, and it's especially different depending on the cast of performers who happen to be there on a given shift. That makes the idea of selling the piece interesting, too. Without documentation, when the piece is reperformed, it will resingularize itself. It will go down really differently. So Sehgal is drawing on the iterative powers of variation I was talking about before, and making something happen that recapitulates the way capitalism and the art market operate, but can also make something not entirely capturable come to pass. Different cultural contexts undoubtedly make a big difference. The bilingual nature of the Montreal performance, and all the etiquette and tensions around which language is used when, certainly made for a singular dynamic in that iteration.

The reason I don't think it works as well for the public is because the effects I'm describing require long duration. They come from the ritualization and repetition – how the piece iterates internally to its own performance. Some people from the public stay for several hours, or come back several times, but most participants stick their head in and leave. They don't stay long enough to get any sense of what manner of event it is. The other thing is that the mechanisms for interpellating the public to speak more often clam them up. It's very intimidating for a lot of people, and when we did it, most people weren't able to respond. But if they stayed, you could often sense them itching to speak, and if you went back to them they did participate. In any case, there is something unresolved in the piece having to do with the performer-public dynamic that left a number of the performers I was in it with feeling that it wasn't really working.

AH: One of the phenomena you are describing reflects the way in which an approach to an aesthetics of duration enables you to activate a strategy of exhaustion. It is that strategy of exhaustion – when there is nothing left to be said between you – that manifests community, that is a fabric-forming, powerfully generative situation.

BM: Yes, because you have to step outside of your normal ways of entering into conversation or into a convivial situation, and reinvent them, without necessarily knowing what will come of it. And yes, the question of duration is really crucial. As you say, there is a certain method of exhaustion built into *This Situation* that has broader implications. Deleuze always said that in order to create you have to first subtract. He's not necessarily referring to the number of elements, it's not a quantitative distinction he's aiming at. What he means by subtracting is putting in suspense the way things normally interconnect and roll onward together, so that there's a moment of rejigging that has to happen for things to start going again. That moment of suspense can invite other tendencies in, and bring other unfoldings about. It's less important to claim to have a solution to problems, like whether the gallery is so compromised that art should go entirely elsewhere, or how to condition the performer-public relation, or whether an artist who sells his or her work is selling out. These questions are too general to be of value. What's important is not coming to supposedly final solutions to general questions. What's important is problematizing – creating singular fields of collective experimentation that make something happen that strikes you as an event, and that offers a relational affordance to others who might want to take up the techniques used, and rework them in their own way, for other situations – a kind of event-variation contagion. That's not about community in the usual sense, but it is about collectivity. It's about collective potentiation that inheres in a fabric of uniquely interwoven events, rather than in any group identity.

Going back to the question of surplus-value, and the distinction I was trying to make between surplus-value of life and the monetary surplus-value of capitalism. I was talking about surplus-value of life as a qualitative excess over functionality, and over capturable utility, as a self-affirming, lived value that it is an end in itself, in a way that doesn't directly feed the capitalist process. A surplus-value of life that is truly uncapturable is, by virtue of that fact, ephemeral. It might return, but each repetition of it is a regeneration, a reinvention, with its own singular vitality affect. The balance shifts toward variation and newness in the sense I was talking about, as an event-quality that is inseparable from the event, and slips away the moment it is reified. So if we're interested in resisting capitalist capture, an important element of that would be to find ways of re-valuing the ephemeral. Capitalism is all about ephemerality, but only as it serves product turnover. Capitalism's interest in ephemerality is about what Schumpeter called "creative destruction." What I'm talking about is ephemerality as part of a process of potentiation. Each singular iteration of an event has contributed a potential to the world that is left in reserve, or in trace form, but as a reactivatable trace. Its newness is renewable, across iterations. What kind of practice could we envision that would be dedicated to the production, storage, and reactivation of event-tracings of this kind? What techniques could be invented for that? And for orienting the iterations politically? There's a term that's become popular that I like a lot: the 'anarchive'. There are a lot of definitions of it. I tend to think of it as an archive of events: an archive that stores only in order to hold an eventful coming-again in reserve, that holds in store for reactivation and variation, not to preserve. The anarchive seems to me to be an important avenue to explore in relation to the question that keeps coming up, of how to resist capitalism given there is no outside of it. Another aspect to grappling with that issue is collectivity. Just as in *This Situation*, when events truly renew themselves, when they are best able to improvise on themselves and invent new variations on their theme, it's because something has been conditioned to occur that's in surplus over the individual contributions. There's an emergent excess that's irreducibly relational, making the collectivity a group-subject. How do you make yourself a group-subject? How do you transmit the conditions that make one emerge? If you succeed in transmitting group-subjecthood, rather than, say, a political platform or an ideology, the potentials are intense. The event-contagion will naturally tend to escape predefined channels, and may turn back against the State and against capitalism. We have seen a number of events in the last few years that have triggered this kind of contagious becoming. The Arab Spring and Occupy are the prime examples. What if we kept experimenting collectively, in whatever context we live or work in, to invent techniques for this kind of self-improvising movement?

AH: I'm wondering if there might be a tension between those two tactics, because one of the things that capital does is to forcibly accelerate processes and time; ephemerality is highly amenable to that acceleration. But I'm wondering if, as a tactic, slow time, slow down, endurance, is actually more affective simply because it runs counter to the temporal organization of capital; the imperative to condense and traverse space, to move ever faster. Or, perhaps the ephemeral strategy, to be effective at all, might be more to do with a tactic of radically multiplying ephemeralities to a point of excess. So a catastrophic speed-up that brings structures, logics and forms to the point of collapse.

BM: There's been a lot of talk recently in philosophy and cultural theory about capitalism as mobilizing circulation of goods, information, people, bodies, and also forms of collaboration, forms of relationality, forms of experience, and pushing them ever further in a tighter and tighter circle, in faster and faster turnover. There is a critique of Deleuze and Guattari coming out of that. Deleuze and Guattari are interpreted as advocating the strategy you just mentioned, as saying that we have to take the tendencies of capitalism further, to the point that the system crashes. This is one version of what is referred to as "accelerationism." But Deleuze and Guattari don't actually say that. What they say is that at that emergent nexus I was talking about before, at the infra-level of event formation, there are tendencies stirring which, if they were fostered and taken to their logical conclusion, would outrun or overspill capitalist capture. They're not talking about taking *capitalism's* tendencies further. They're talking about *counter-tendencies* to capitalism that are infra-, or immanent, to capitalism's process – but not its system. They're not in the way capitalism orders or regulates itself, or fails to effectively, they're in its conditions of emergence – which, going back to our earlier discussion, do not resemble it. The immanent counter-tendencies stirring at the emergent level are by nature self-affirming, unless they're captured or preempted. They are self-validating, and create their own experiential value. What they "want" is to run to their fullest expression, and capitalist capture curtails that. So they're off-kilter to the capitalist system, which is not monolithic. It's global, even universal in a sense, but it's not monolithic. It's too adaptable, too transmutable, and too wily in its transmutations, for that. Which is another reason why it's not reducible to a structure or a system, that it's a process. Anyway, it's the off-kilteredness that you have to push further, not the tendencies of capitalism, even its own potentially suicidal mania for acceleration and faster and faster turnover feeding the production of its monetary form of surplus-value. When capitalism crashes, it carries countless lives down with it. The accelerationist strategy is playing with fire, and it's not the relatively privileged proponents of that doctrine who would get burned the most. The idea I'm suggesting is that you can meet capitalism strategically on the ground to which it returns to renew and reenable itself, that is to say its field of emergence. That field is rife with germinal potentials of all kinds which are not capitalistic per se – capitalism wouldn't have to "capture" tendencies if they weren't liable to escape. The idea is to find a way to return to that terrain of emergence otherwise, spiking the potential differently, fostering different kinds of tendencies oriented toward the production of self-affirming surplus-values of life that answer to a purely qualitative economy, multiplying and accelerating that *escape* from capitalism, that leak from it.

AH: Many of the examples of semblance phenomena and vitality affects we have been discussing have a movement content: the mouse that runs at the edge of perception whose trajectory you feel, the dog whose bark arrives before it arrives, and the crashing vehicle, which carries a very paradoxical temporality, at once too fast and too slow. So: a little constellation of relations between the human-animal, the animal and the machine. Thinking about the relationship between movement and politics: we are the animals that have a very particular historical imperative in relation to movement. As modern subjects we are supposed to move, to use our tools and machines to eliminate the limitations of movement, to keep moving. Movement is not neutral or benign, but pre-conditioned by powers. Part of the consequence of that movement imperative politically is not very good, let's say for instance, ecologically in terms of these relations between human-animals and other animals, between humans and the planet. I'm wondering whether in relationship to politics, or to aesthetics, what's actually really imperative is to find forms of movement that are self-questioning, or self-annulling; that it is movement itself that must be interrogated as a prior organizing condition of subjectivity.

BM: I think you're absolutely right that it is precisely movement that needs to be interrogated, but it's not an either/or between moving or not moving, because there's no such thing as rest. Whitehead talks about one of the basic metaphysical concepts being a "principle of unrest." This dovetails with the idea of what I call an activist philosophy – a philosophy for which the fundamental concept is activity. As I was saying earlier, there's always movement going on, of some kind, at some level. So movement *or* rest is not the question, but rather economies of movement *and* rest, by which I mean rhythms of movement, modes of movement, patterns of cut and continuity, of arising and perishing, and of the experiential qualities associated with those modes. There's thinking and experimenting that needs to be done on how to counteract mechanisms of capture that we think of as stilling. Like the way a self-organizing political movement so often gets rechanneled into traditional politics, as happened last year to the 2012 Quebec student movement, which was on the verge of veering in explicitly anticapitalist directions when an election was called in response to the student demands. The movement got immediately rechanneled into electoral politics at that point. That was certainly a capture. But it wasn't a stoppage of the movement, it was a channeling of movement. The enormous energy and potential the movement had released was channeled into a different mode of activity, on a different level. The students "won" on their immediate macropolitical demand – tuition was not increased. But they lost their movement. The new government took it, and dissipated it. But there's always something that continues across any capture, on what Deleuze and Guattari call the *micropolitical* level.

Despite the term, it actually doesn't mean politics on a smaller scale, although it can be, and in general it's easier to get it moving on smaller scales. What it actually refers to is imperceptibility. The micropolitical can occur at any scale, but wherever it is, it passes unrecognized. It isn't caught in the usual filters of activity and structures of understanding, because it embodies a singular mode of movement that's too ghostly or slippery for that. "Micropolitical" refers to a quality of movement – a movement doubled by its own semblance and resonating with the potential of that intensification. Deleuze and Guattari define the State as an "apparatus of capture" (1987: 424-473). It captures and channels, in order to slow things down and dissipate untoward potentials. Capitalism, on the other hand, captures in order to speed them up, for its own purposes. It mobilizes – but it's important not to reduce movement to mobilization. The crucial point is that an apparatus of capture has to wait for things to start moving on their own before it can capture them and feed off them. It has to wait until the movements afoot become perceptible to it, so that it can apply its mechanisms to it. This isn't just a question of scale. Occupy was "imperceptible" to traditional politics, in the sense that it just didn't compute. What, no leaders? No demands? Group mechanisms of enunciation, like the human microphones? Something's going on here, but what it was totally escaped the grasp of those, on the Left or the Right, who think in terms of the traditional macropolitics of political programs, representation, and recognizable forms of advocacy. Occupy was not following a program. It was embodying the principle of unrest. It was operating on the germinal level of event-formation. For the participants, this did generate a surplus-value of life, a self-affirming qualitative intensity of the kind you don't often get to experience, and that never really leaves you. It leaves its traces. I can say that for certain, thinking back on my own formative involvement in the anti-nuclear movement in the 1970s and 1980s and the direct-action anarchist collectives I was working with and living with. It leaves traces, and the micropolitical unrest comes back, in other forms and other contexts, in imperceptible ways. So in the end, I don't consider Occupy or the Quebec student movement as failures. They succeeded in the way micropolitical movements always succeed. They feed potential forward, into the iterative event-fabric of life. You can feel a palpable change in Montreal since the student movement, a bubbling of energies and political imagination that you would never know was there if you weren't attuned to it. It certainly doesn't show up at the level of macropolitical debates, or in the media.

There's no general rule, or sure-fire techniques for micropolitics. Slowness can be extremely useful given the acceleration of the mobilizing tendencies, but there are other ways of becoming imperceptible. It's more about qualities of movement than speed.

AH: When they arise in social bodies or movements, these micropolitical tactics that you've been speaking of work a lot through differentiation, and through dissensus, through amorphous collective agency. Is there a tension or a redundancy when one moves to the macropolitical, which seems to need to work through consensus, through whole identifiable agents who activate things in the world, who stake claim to projects that have objectives?

BM: Yes, there's a difference in mode of organization, mode of activity, between the macropolitical and the micropolitical. What characterizes the macropolitical is that it has a central or general organizing principle, which it tries to apply. That implies that what effectively organizes the field of relation, the social field, is somehow separable from it. The principle of organization comes from above, and then swoops down in order to make what happens on ground level conform with it, channel into its mechanism, and to pacify it. It is the anti-principle-of-unrest. It often has a representational mode of operating. Another characteristic is that macropolitics thinks in terms of bounded wholes, bounded unities. It is always concerned, even obsessed, with setting the boundary between the inside and the outside. This is even true of the most liberal democracy. To say that a representative democracy is "inclusive" presupposes a boundary that you cross to come in, which amounts to implicitly admitting that there have been exclusions. You just have to look at the way migration and refugee issues are playing out in Europe and North America to see how fundamental the notion of the social field as a bounded whole is to the macropolitical State.

At the micropolitical level, things are very different. For one thing, the principle of unrest rises up, it doesn't swoop down. It emerges into determinate expression. At the micropolitical level, there's a multiplication of differentiations and a vagueness that's not a simple lack of definition, but an overfullness with potential. Whatever emerges from that germinal reality takes on a clarity and a precision where something determinate happens. But that's just a region of clarity surrounded by a penumbra of potentials held in reserve, in trace form. There's a fringe or periphery that goes out in all directions, full of tendencies that have not been actualized, but might be at another moment, under different conditions. These potential movements might even infect or inflect what clearly happens without ever being actualized, just by exerting a pressure of potential. So the micropolitical field is a constitutively open multiplicity populated by tendencies and potentials, not subjects or objects. The macropolitical has a structural unity, it sets down boundaries and accretes centres of power, centres for the deployment of an order to which everything is called upon to conform. These centres of decision can be democratic in the representative sense, or they could be dictatorial. They can be distributed throughout the social field, or centralized in a monolithic State. The structural unity could even conceivably organize itself through a friendly consensus-based democracy. But then it could just as well be a fascism that gets so obsessed with policing the boundary of what's in and what gets excluded that it turns murderous. The macropolitical is itself a tendency that takes many forms of expression. But there is always the concern for the boundedness of the field of relation. For macropolitics, everything within that field must be well identified and defined, it has to have an assignable position in a structure of power. On the micropolitical level, on the other hand, there is always a surplus of organization, or better, organizability: a surplus-value of life stirring in the between of positioned things, moving to take its own form of expression, self-organizing and self-affirming. Broadly, micropolitics corresponds to what macropolitical discourse dismisses as the pipe-dream of "direct democracy." I prefer to think of it as the nightmare of the State.

AH: Can I ask you then about the role, the function of belief, faith and hope in the political? When you laid a name to the operations of the micropolitical as "a pragmatics of potential," you framed this as neither being buoyed by false hope, nor paralyzed by hopelessness. I'm wondering about the nature and necessity of belief and hope for political transformation. Is it not the case that people, political subjects, need to feel that they have found belief, that belief is not necessarily an automatism, something just happening to them, but that an important political agency arises from a sense of "ownership" over their beliefs?

BM: I wouldn't put it in those terms, because I think that in moments of change, we're immersed in a relational field where actions are so closely intertwined that it's very hard to separate out an agent. There's a kind of field-effect that means that factors combine, fuse, enter into tension, so that what happens, happens between, in the complexity of it. So if you talk about what the political subject needs, I think you're already making the transition toward the macropolitical level. The concept of belief is very problematic for me because it brings the political back into the interiority of the subject. The concept of hope is similarly problematic. It addresses individual aspirations, even if it's often in the name of a coming-together. What I think is needed in political action is not a hope, but a way. Ways of continuing to move, continuing to be implicated with others in activities that have their own value, their end in themselves, just by virtue of the quality of experience that they give. I think more in terms of intensity, intensities of relation, than of hope. As we saw with the

2008 Obama presidential campaign, hope can be an extremely powerful mobilizing force. But it is just that, a mobilizing force, not a self-organizing movement. A mobilizing force is a sovereign force, a power-over. At any rate, the mobilization of hope is guaranteed to disappoint because it promises some sort of lasting solution. It's a kind of redemptive gesture. But in this world there is no redemption. There's only the intensity of the ongoing, with the variations that eventuate. Instead of offering hope, what I think needs to be done is to experiment with techniques enabling people to reconnect with relational fields that yield enhanced intensity, that produce surplus-value of life expressing themselves in emergent forms of organization and experience. As these movements grow and proliferate, it is inevitable that at some point they will confront macropolitical obstacles. If the technique is there, they may even be able to assert solutions to macropolitical questions while refusing capture, while refusing to abandon their own micropolitical quality, tendencies, and penchant for escape.

This is where a concept of belief can come back in. But it doesn't have to do with belief in a political program, or belief in an ideology or doctrine. There are other forms of belief that you could think about. For example, at the incipient level I've been talking about, the germinal level of any event, I think it's more the case that you find yourself again in an event, rather than that you believe in something and get there following your belief. It's related to the kinds of interruptions and ruptures we were talking about when I was saying that we're braced into an event before we have a chance to cognize a path, or stop and choose where we are going. That bracing into the event happens so quickly that our cognizance of it is always at a slight remove, at a slight lag, so that by the time we are in a reflective mode of assessing and choosing, we're already out of the event, in its future. In the moment, there is no act of judgment that occurs separate from the in-bracing – which as we saw, was already a form of thinking, considering the abstractness of the semblance, and the immediate comprehension of potentials and alternate outcomes it envelops. In the event, there is no doubt. There's no possibility of doubt, because you're already in a movement you're going to have no choice but to ride out. The event is compulsory. That doesn't mean the outcome is predestined, and that there is no freedom. The coming of the event carries imperatives, but it also carries potential, possibilities for improvisation and change. The freedom we have is to modulate its unfolding, from within that very unfolding, at no reflective distance, in the immediacy of our thinking-feeling of what is happening as it ushers into action. Connecting thinking-feelingly, at no remove from the event, to the aspects of the event that carry potential is a kind of belief. It's what Deleuze called a *"belief in this world"* – a faith that the world has always more to offer, if only we ride its waves with intensity and technique. This has nothing to do with a belief in a doctrine, or a belief in a representation of the world, certainly not a belief in another world. It's a lived belief in this world, in this world's richness, its changeability, it's capacity to offer intensity and surplus-value of life. This is a belief that is one with our active, intensely feeling and thinking participation in the world. So I think more in terms of intensifying that, finding methods, techniques for furthering it. So in that sense, yes, there's a place for a certain notion of belief, or even of faith. But it's more a form of intuition than a form of conscious belief in the normal sense. There's no adherence in this kind of belief. You don't believe in, you're in your belief, with every dawning thought and act.

AH: I'd love to hear more about reactivating a notion of intuition, either in relation to art practice or in relation to political activism. In relation to art practice it has been such a degraded term, partly because of its association with the holding of transcendent powers and the mystification of processes, and in activism I'm not sure how it would even begin to operate as a notion. Had you thoughts on that?

BM: Yeah... the concept of intuition comes up for me because of my particular background, coming out of Bergson. Bergson defines intuition as the "lowering of the barriers of space" in such a way that we're "transported into the heart of the object" in a condition of absolute "sympathy" with it (Bergson 1998: 177; translation modified). For that to work for me, given my process philosophy bias, I need to strike "object" and replace it with "event." And I need to rethink "sympathy" as something that is not in the interiority of a subject. Sympathy is rather "the relational activity constitutive of the event," the formative activity of the event's arising. The clichéd idea of intuition as a bolt of inspiration that hits the individual has nothing to do with it. Sympathy in the sense I was just talking about is collective – or better, transindividual, to use Simondon's term. So if the barriers of space lower in relation to the formative activity of an event, what that means is that you have a direct prehension (to avoid the term cognition) – an immediate, active grasp – of what may come of the event on all sides. You're not just thinking-feeling it from your point of view. Because you're in the middle, where actions and formative factors are intersecting at the level of their tendencies. You're in the potential filling the gaps between the tendencies. There, you can't be in your subject position, because who or what you will be will play out of a function of how the intersecting tendencies shake down. You're not in your subject position, you're in becoming. Sympathy in this sense has nothing to do with the human emotion of empathy. It's not a human emotion. It's a state of the world, at a point of rupture or discontinuity – when the dust settles, things will be different. Sympathy is the immediate embodied enactive understanding of the potentials coming out of that field of relation, from the angle of this differencing.

AH: Wouldn't that be braided with multiple emotions though? Why distinguish that feeling, that prehension from the emotive?

BM: Yes, it is braided with all kinds of affects. Normally there's a dominant affect that is unrefuseable, that takes you in, and in which you have no choice but to believe, because that's just the quality of what's happening. That's what Whitehead calls the "affective tonality" that imposes itself at the beginning of an event, and marks the transition from the last event into this one. He uses the example of anger. When your life partner gets angry at you, you don't have to stop and think about what kind of event this is. You feel it, unmistakeably. You already know that you're in an anger-event, and there's no way to unchoose being there, you have to deal with it. At that moment, the anger is much more than an emotion. It's colored by any number of other emotions – shame, love, a desire for reconciliation. What we think of as an emotion is an affective nexus. It always envelops a whole spectrum, just as every color on the spectrum is inhabited by other colors. It's only after the event that you can tie up the nexus neatly enough to fit into a single category, and leave behind the fullness with immediate spectrum of feeling, which can be frightful because of its intensity, and destabilizing because of its multipleness. The reason to say "affect" rather than "emotion" is that affect carries a bodily connotation. Affect, coming out of Spinoza, is defined very basically as the ability to affect and be affected. But you have to think of the affect and being affected together as a complex, as two sides of the same phenomenon that cuts across subject positions. You are affected by anger, but you also affect it in return, for example by stiffening up to repel it or to brace for a fight. Your affecting your being-affected-by the anger immediately affects the other person. The force of their anger has shifted, and with it the potentials they have in that situation. Affect escapes the active-passive opposition, and it always directly operates transindividually. The bodily dimension is that the feelings this transindividual affective nexus carry envelop incipient actions, they're already incipient actions. When you bristle in the face of another's anger you stiffen as in anticipation of a punch. The other's anger has already hit like an inhibited punch, it carried germs of punching that were not allowed to unfold, but still hit you with an abstract force. Semblances can hurt. That's why the concept of affect is so fundamental to an activist philosophy. It gives you a way of thinking about emotion, and other things we take to be interior and subjective, in terms of activity and movements in the world.

AH: There is then never "an emotion" at all, in a unitary sense: emotion is always already shot through with immense multiplicities, paradoxes and contradictions?

BM: That's right. There is no unity of emotion. Affectively, we're always talking about multiplicities. Politically, thinking on this affective, germinal level of events in the making suggests that we can create collective platforms for experimentation at the level of our shared belief in the world. In other words, we can experiment with techniques that bring people together, leaving behind their subject positions, suspending their personal beliefs, their doctrines, but bringing with them *what moves them*. What forces them to think, what forces them to act, their passions, their techniques, their competencies, all of that brought as a kind of gift, not to others, so much as to their interaction, to the event that's brewing between. A germinal politics.

3

Collective Expression: A Radical Pragmatics

> Now it is undeniably conceivable that a beginningless series of successive utterers should all do their work in a brief interval of time, and that so should an endless series of interpreters. Still, it is not likely to be denied that, in some cases, neither the series of utterers nor that of interpreters forms an infinite collection. When this is the case, there must be a sign without an utterer and a sign without an interpreter. ... Neither an utterer, nor even, perhaps, an interpreter is essential to a sign. ... I am led to inquire whether there be not some ingredient of the utterer and some ingredient of the interpreter which not only are so essential, but are even more characteristic of signs than the utterer or interpreter themselves.
>
> C.S. Peirce (1998: 403-404)

A Technique

1. Choose a generative text.
2. Choose a minor concept weaving through the generative text.
3. Ask each person in the group to count off as a one or a two.
4. Instruct the ones that they are "posts."

5. Instruct the twos that they are "flows."

6. Ask the posts to find a post: a spot in the room where they would like to have a conservation.

7. Ask the flows to pair up with a post.

8. Direct everyone to a page in the text where the minor concept occurs.

9. Ask the participants to discuss the function of the minor concept, staying as close as possible to the text, with detailed attention to how it is constructed.

10. Notify participants that when exactly five minutes are up they will hear a signal, and that when they hear the signal they must end their conversation immediately, even if they are in the middle of a word.

11. When the five-minute signal sounds, ask all flows to move to the next post in a clockwise direction.

12. Repeat eight to ten times.

13. Bring the group back together and discuss in plenary session what was discovered about the minor concept and the text.

This is "conceptual speed dating." It is a technique that has been practiced at the SenseLab for ten years, and has been adapted by a number of its participants for classroom use. Its introduction at the SenseLab[1] was motivated by the disappointments of plenary discussions of assigned texts. Full-group discussions predispose participants to perform themselves – their own already-acquired knowledge or interpretive virtuosity – at the expense of truly exploratory thinking-together in the moment, for the collective movement forward into follow-up activities. Self-performance can quickly have the effect of silencing those whose practice is not primarily text-oriented or language-based, as is the case of the majority of SenseLab participants with backgrounds in dance and movement, materials-based creative processes, and media art. It also skews participation along gender lines and according to personality traits like shyness. The quality of the interaction tends to suffer as well from a conversational birth defect: the scourge of generality. It is difficult to keep a large group focused on the specificity of the text before it. In the absence of an effective anchoring in the singularity of the thinking process embodied in the text, the discussion quickly slips into comparison. Given the diversity of backgrounds, the comparative allusions inevitably reference texts or bodies of knowledge known only to a few of those present. In an attempt to overcome the divide, the discussion will invariably start to pivot on hinge words that seem at the same time to offer a common ground for understanding and to illuminate some aspect of the text at hand: "history," "culture," "nature," "life," "matter," "space, "time." It could be just about anything, but "subject" and "object" always figure, bringing in tow a host of others. The problem is that the force of these terms actually differ substantially from discipline to discipline, and even from text to text within a discipline. The differences hover in the background, unspoken, their mute presence creating an illusion that speakers' remarks are actually intersecting, when a little scratching below the surface reveals that they are passing each other in the ether-sea of generality like phantom ships on a low-budget cruise. Missed encounter. The unacknowledged mutual incomprehension appears as difference of opinion, and the missed encounter is experienced as debate. What is actually accomplished is an object lesson in why Deleuze always said that the greatest enemy of thought is conversation, understood as the exchange of individual ideas and opinions. In a word, communication. The aim of the technique of conceptual speed dating is to address the group-dynamics problems of the plenary discussion format, while disenabling the tendency to default to the communicational model of verbal performance and its general sea-sickness.

The conceptual speed dating technique assumes that the text under consideration is "generative." By this is meant that no one reading can exhaust its potential for producing meaning. Each return to the text, even by the same reader, will crystallize new thoughts. One way of thinking about this generative capacity is to approach the key concepts of the text as nexuses composed of a number of conceptual lines entering into constellations of varying emphasis, certain of them rising into relief at what stand out as key passages. The particular force of these passages is synthetic, leaping out from the weave of the text as a joint effect of the contributory lines. The constellations dissolve, reform, and reconstellate around each other's emphases as the text advances. What stands out at key passages, or in the same key passage that commends itself to attention in successive readings, moves and varies. The variation is related to many factors, not all of them internal to the text: the reader's level of attention, how his or her understanding has been primed by the experience of the day, how knowledge and experience accumulated since the last reading informs the reading, and even (or, as we will see, especially) by modulations of attention and concern by the situation in which the reading or discussion is taking place. A generative text is constitutively open to its outside. It does not just transmit significations. It welcomes inflections. It is hospitable to new thought. This puts its meaning always in-the-making, making the meaning inexhaustible. A generative text is never done.

The openness of the generative text to its outside must not be reduced to a question of reception. The reader is not adding meaning to a finished text. S/he is entering the unfinishment of the text, and drawing from it a new determination. The text's power of variation is as *composed* within as it is inflected from without. In the synthetic meaning-effect of a given constellation, the relevance of the contributory conceptual lines is graded. Many register less noticeably, some barely register at all. Many more do not register at all – yet are still positively contributory in virtue of how their avoidance affords other conceptual lines a chance to shine. These shaded conceptual lines are what we refer to, for the purposes of conceptual speed dating, as "minor" concepts.

It is crucial to the success of the conceptual speed dating technique that the concept chosen for the exercise be a minor concept. What rises into relief at a key passage stands out from the weave of the text in a way that can be misunderstood as detaching itself from the text to claim general validity. If a danger-word, like "nature" or "subject," occurs in the passage or is even just implied by it, the risk is extreme that the discussion will cruise into general waters. When this happens, the minor concept assumes "major" status. Major concepts, those of the general, communication-ready kind, must be avoided at all costs if the technique is to work. It is always the case that a minor concept will also be present. This is one that a reader may well not have noticed. But once attention is drawn to it, it becomes palpable how integral it is to the passage, and that the passage could not have worked its effect without it. It is also always the case that the minor concept will recur, explicitly or implied, in other passages, making it an essential, if underappreciated, contributor to the warp and weft of the entire text. Analysis of the minor concept and its textual weave offers a singular angle of approach to the text as a whole, from which new thoughts are more apt to emerge. The process of working the minor increases the sensitivity of the text to its outside, and particularly to modulations owing to the particularities of the situation of the reading and discussion. This is because major concepts carry dead weight. They are laden with baggage that exerts an inertial resistance against effective variation. Minor concepts, once noticed, are self-levitating. Once the ballast of the general ideas is thrown overboard, minor concepts' sensitivity to the outside, coupled with their intimateness to the compositional weave composing the text, makes them rise.

In the practice of the SenseLab, the most generative concepts are philosophical concepts. Approached as generative, even the abstractest, seemingly hermetic texts, rise and fly. Conceptual speed dating with philosophical texts is used by the SenseLab for the purpose of collectively "activating" minor concepts. The collectivity is key. The project of the SenseLab is to experiment with event-based modes of creative collaboration cutting across the established boundaries between disciplines, and between "theory" (language work) and "practice" (movement, materials or media-based work). For this to happen, the collaboration cannot be conceived of as a meeting-place of constituted methods, or even of individuals. The individuals involved, and whatever they bring to the event in terms of already-acquired knowledge, skills and approaches, must enter a space of relation whose complexion does not preexist the event, but emerges from the encounter – meaning that the "space" of the event is a space-time singular to it. The space-time of the event is not located in individual actions. It is in the interstices between them. It is inhabited as the environment of the interaction, as well as emerging from it. It is a third, interstitial space, irreducible to the sum of individual inputs. "Collectivity," in the SenseLab context, does not mean the aggregate of individual actions. It means what cannot be ascribed to individual actions, taken separately or in aggregate –but would not arise without them.

In conceptual speed dating, the focus on close reading of the text, together with a '"minor" sensitivity to the situation, helps produce the conditions for the emergence of a space-time of active relation. Close reading is requisite. The question asked of the minor concept is how it helps *make* the text, and helps it mean what it says, ever in excess of any settled meaning that might be ascribed to it by a disciplinary reading. Approaching the text through the minor concept is a way of asking the text what it *does*, and how it does what it does, compositionally. If instead of starting with these minor questions, the discussion moves too quickly to comparison or critique, the potential for active relation is lost. Comparison begins by assuming a commonality between texts. This in turn assumes that there are certain overarching concepts that apply to both texts, and against which the adequacy of each text can be assessed. Comparison begins with the sameness of the conceptually already-given. Minor reading looks to the text's potential differencing: its capacity to exceed the givenness of ideas – especially its own. Critique, for its part, begins by separating the reader from the text so that he or she may stand over and apart from it as judge. From the lofty height of judgment's peak, the minoritarian texture of the text fades into a feature-poor, homogenized expanse. Only stand-out concepts, telescoped to the general level, remain in view. This kills the potential movement of the text's thinking even before it begins. SenseLab reading groups take place under the sign of a priori sympathetic reading, as expressed in a famous quote by Bertrand Russell (literally – a large-scale printout of the quote is often hung in the room):

> In studying a philosopher, the right attitude is neither reverence nor contempt, but first a kind of hypothetical sympathy, until it is possible to know what it feels like to believe in his theories, and only then a revival of the critical attitude, which should resemble, as far as possible, the state of mind of a person abandoning opinions which he has hitherto held. (Russell 1996: 47)

Directing participants toward a close, textural reading of how the text means helps disable the default positions of comparison and critique. It also helps lessen the silencing effect that might otherwise take hold due to differences in background, gender, and social ease, by literally putting everybody on the same page. When discussion is oriented toward the detail of what is in the text, and everyone has the text in front of them, the hump someone has to get over to make a contribution is significantly lowered. In close-reading practices, the first question is not "how does this compare to other ways of thinking with which I am more familiar but others may not be?" or "how am I going to position myself in relation to this, given where I'm coming from?" The first question is: what page is that on? What concepts co-occur there? On what other pages do they reoccur, and do they re-co-occur in those passages in the same constellation, or do they go off on their own trajectories and just check with a congerie of others from time to time? If the latter, where are those other trajectories leading?

In not a few cases, they will turn out not to lead anywhere. A conceptual line of development has embedded itself in the text which the text was not willing or able to follow through on. This amounts to the discovery of a seed of thought planted in the text that did not fully germinate in it. These germinal thought-lines are not gratuitous. They are necessary contributors to the weave of the text. They are in a certain way affirmed by the text, even though they are not fully assumed by it. They are *thought tendencies* that the text needs – but that it needs not to follow in order to remain the text the author generally understood it to be. They are thought *potential* that the text has planted on its own soil, but that needs new soil to flourish. Minoritarian close reading seizes upon these seeds of thought potential. Where might it lead if one of those trajectories were assumed, were fully activated and followed through to their logical conclusion? They lead into new territories of thought, beyond the ken of the text's author him- or herself. Exploring these tendencies is a way of remaining radically faithful to the letter of the text, avoiding the pitfalls of comparison and critique, without being boxed in by it. What occurs, rather than comparison or critique, is an *immanent conversion* of the text by way of its own thought tendencies. Gilles Deleuze's books on other philosophers are prominent examples of this process of immanent conversion, taking the text where the author couldn't take it, by excess of faithfulness to its texture. This can be seen, for instance, in Deleuze's book on Bergson, where an episode in Bergson's thought in which matter and memory (mind) lose their opposition to one another and place themselves on the same continuum as different degrees of the same variation. Deleuze seizes upon this moment as a germinal tendency, then takes that tendency to its logical conclusion, yielding a Bergson no one before had suspected, different from all other Bergsons, including Bergson's Bergson, but no less Bergsonian for that –on the contrary, all the more so.

The technique of conceptual speed dating is designed to stage a collective encounter between a group of readers and a text, at the point where each side is *outdoing* itself: participants are brought out of their personal opinions, preestablished positions, and expert identities, at the same time as the text is made to outpace itself with its own tendencies. At that point, a power of thought that cannot be reduced to either the text or the readers as an aggregate of individuals is released as a vector: a creative vector in the direction of new thought. This can be achieved without the speed dating technique, for example through a sustained reading-group practice based on a dedication to "hypothetical sympathy," safeguarded by a culture of that kind of reading, an ethos tended by all involved.

It is at the point of the text's and the readers' mutual outdoing that concepts are activated. In SenseLab practice, "activating" concepts means outdoing them in such a way that they fly off from their textual homes and migrate to other modes of activity whose primary medium is not language, thereby crossing the supposed theory/practice divide. The first time the technique was used at *Dancing the Virtual* (2005), one of the texts we read was William James' "The World of Pure Experience" from *Essays in Radical Empiricism* (1996). Rather than concentrating on a major concept such as "experience" or "consciousness," the minor concept of "terminus" was chosen. This is a concept that to our knowledge had never been focused upon in the literature on James and radical empiricism as a full-fledged philosophical concept. In James' text, the terminus is the end of a process, as it is present to the process in anticipation. In other words, it is an attractor pole that lies at the limit of a movement, but dynamizes it from within as that which the movement tends toward. Although it exerts a formative force on the process, operating immanently to it, the terminus does not actually exist for the process until it is reached and the process makes done with itself. The terminus is realized by the process and actually exists only as realized by that very movement toward it. The terminus is effectively *created* by the movement tending toward it, giving it a strange status of future-past. A James different from all other Jameses, including his own, comes with seizing upon the terminus as a tendency. For this terminally reactivated James, the virtual – that which exerts a formative force without being actual – becomes key to the understanding of pragmatism (of which radical empiricism is the metaphysical correlate for James). Everything changes when pragmatism is seen to revolve around the formative force of the virtual, rather than the obligation of utility. Everything changes, but nothing so much as our sense of what "practice" means.

The speed dating with the concept of the terminus at *Dancing the Virtual* activated the notions of immanent formative force, tendential unfolding toward attractor poles, the ability of that tendency to actually create its own end, the future-pastness of that creativity, and the abstractness (virtuality) of the motor of the movement toward it. In the follow-up materials-based practice session, these seeded concepts were *enacted*: they recurred to the group in the form of embodied interactions. How does the terminus work in dance improvisation? How does it work in everyday perception? Small groups invented a number of variations on what happens when the concept of the terminus becomes immanently formative of embodied action. The small groups were then invited to bring the result of their experimentation back to the whole group. They were asked not to report on what had happened. No description from a distance. No conversation. No comparison or (self-) critique.

They were asked instead to *perform* it anew, in a way adapted to the larger group: to reactivate it again. This ignited a series of reenactments that continued, themselves becoming an formative force immanent to the three-day event's trajectory. The terminus became the refrain of the event. Its serial actings-out in-formed the reading of the other texts the group read together. The terminus migrated from text to embodied action and back again, eventually spinning out from the event to take on a life of its own. The concept became a formative factor in the writing practice of a number of SenseLab participants (including myself), and the tendency toward it still regularly returns to in-form SenseLab activities foregrounding media other than language. A formative potential was planted that continues to grow and vary.

As this example shows, activating a concept does not just lead to new thoughts, but extends to new actions as well, and to the new perceptions that new actions allow to unfold. How to *do* things with words ... How to make language and non-language-based activities enter in symbiosis, without one side lording it over the other. How to *transduce* a conceptual force incumbent in language into a full-body enactive potential that can act itself out. And vice versa. Once the transductive circuit is set going, the in-formative movement is two-way. It is just as possible to start with a making that privileges a material other than language and then go on to generate concept-formation follow-on effects as it is to start with textual concept work and move into its embodied acting-out. This two-way processual reciprocity lies at the heart of the SenseLab's discourse/practice of "research-creation" (the Canadian term for art-based research).

The very experience of conceptual speed dating is a lesson in itself. The first five-minute exchange or two are often spent orienting to the conceptual problem, reading the initial passage that had been indicated looking for pointers, moving up and down from it to get a sense of the lay of the textual land. The change from one exchange to the next creates a cesura that raises the question of how to rebegin. One party may ask what had come of the other party's last exchange. Or, buoyed by an unexpected realization, one of the parties may immediately set the agenda, with a sense of urgency to make further progress before the bell rings. The sounding of the signal to change partners always feels as though it has come at an inopportune time, either because it come before a good connection was made between the interlocutors, or for the opposite reason, because an intense connection was made but didn't have time to reach the end of its arc. After a few changes of partner, the cesuras between the exchanges begin to feel less and less like interruptions. Strands of discussion hang in the air, not neutralized but pressing to continue, with different degrees of urgency. An odd sensation builds that the texture of the discussion's *continuity* fills the intervals, vaguely but insistently felt as the co-pressing of lines of thought. In the cesura, they are intimately interwound. But over the threshold to the next exchange, it goes without saying that they will separate out, before re-interwinding. Each cesura is filled with the resonation of the many lines of thought, jostling each other, each vying to follow its own trajectory further, sometimes in a mutually reinforcing way, at other times in interference. Some will fall into the gap, failing to reemerge in the next exchange, fallen mute. Mute but not inert. They will have a mark, of some kind, somewhere, and it is never a foregone conclusion that they will not revive later, perhaps elsewhere. What does not flourish, nevertheless seeds itself.

Speaking personally, by the midway point of the exercise, what I say as I enter the next exchange ceases to feel as if it came from a separate decision made by me. What I say feels moved by the necessity of a particularly pressing strand that takes my tongue for a ride. The result often surprises me. I find myself saying things I hadn't plan to say, or hadn't been able to say before. Sometimes I'm not even sure I agree with them. But rather than being alienating, that feeling intensifies the sensation of being *in* the disussion. Owning a thought personally and expressing an opinion has simply ceased to be what is at stake. What is at stake is a *movement of thought* passing through the exchanges and rolling with the intervals. The felt imperative is to be true not to oneself but to that movement: to help further its iterative unfolding, toward a terminus whose contours are unknown in their details, but whose presence is effective: compelling (another iteration) and orienting (giving a sense of direction). The vagueness of the terminus does not feel like an absence. It feels creative. Whatever series of exchanges lead further in its direction will have to construct the path it will follow toward it. By the end, I have the odd sensation of having had an experience full of thought, but without being able to say who it was who actually thought it up. Thinking of a particular point that arose, I often cannot remember if it was I who had that thought, or another who passed it on to me. I feel as though I have been *in* thought – rather than the thoughts having been in me.[2] The plenary session following the final speed dating exchange is permeated by this feeling, giving each person's utterance a flavor of indirect discourse – under conditions in which it is impossible to single out the author of the reported speech.

Who is speaking? Me, my interlocutors, the text itself? In this event, where did thought begin and end? The initial suggestion of the minor concept to be discussed is not really where the thinking began. "Life" – the life of thought, and living thinking – "begins only at the point where utterance crosses utterance" (Vološinov 1986: 145). In other words: in the cesuras between individual speakings. The thinking originated in the multiplicity of its speed-dated rebeginnings. The event generated its own effective origin, immanent to its occurrence. The initial suggestion was only the pretext for this immanent origin, which is one with the articulations of the event. This is what Simondon calls an "absolute origin" (Simondon 1969: 57). The initial gesture that gives the thought to come its pretext is but its jumping off point. The origination of thought is in the event-articulations where utterance crosses utterance, in serial interations interwinding. The origin is not a first time: it is time and again. It parses the event into separate episodes, rising in each cesura's fall into silence. It inhabits the event, immanent to the event's occurrence, the overall effect of which is not attributable to any one gesture or any one participant, or even to the sum total of the participants considered in their individual inputs. It all amounts to an eventful self-reporting of thought, indistinguishable from its multiply authored occurrence, arising from its distributed "absolute" origin.

A successful conceptual speed dating session will bear the same relation to a follow up session that each of its constituent exchanges bore to each other. What flourished and what self-seeded will co-inhabit the interval, and what presses forward from it will be conditioned by the nature of the initializing gesture that will be the jumping off point of the next event. If the initiating conditions for the next event are couched in movement rather than language, the lines of thought will press for whole-body enactment, activated and oriented by the same terminus, continuing the same tendency in a different materiality, the phonic movement of thought in language transduced into a full-spectrum embodied thinking in movement. The movement that arises from the next collective exercise will have been in-formed by the preceding movement of thought in language, as by an immanent formative force. A return to language further down the line will in-form language, reactivated and reoriented by movement. At that point, it is no longer possible to assign either language or movement as the origin to the unfolding. Thinking will have outdone itself. It will have tendentially spread.

This is the cross-practice equivalent of free indirect discourse. Thinking self-reports cross-wise. It "says" itself multiply, across words and movement (and images and sounds; and bodily gesture and verbalization). But through that multiplicity, it says itself of a single process of "absolutely" original articulation: a creative movement, single in its occurrence. For the SenseLab, this transductive relay, this singular cross-articulate expression of thought eventfully self-reporting, is what best characterizes what research-creation can do.

It is conceivable, Peirce was saying in the opening quote, that a beginningless series of successive utterers should all do their work in a brief interval of time, and that so should an endless series of interpreters. But it gets really interesting, he continues, when neither the series of utterers nor that of interpreters forms an infinite collection. When the set is finite there will be signs without utterers or interpreters. It is precisely at these points that expression asserts its *autonomy*. Thought (or what from the point of view of the theory of the signs necessary for its enactment Peirce names "semiosis") will have become its own self-creative movement.

A Pragmatics

Peirce's emphasis on *finitude* when talking about the self-propagating power of thought, apparently limitless in its autonomous cross-power to relay itself, seems paradoxical at first sight. But it makes perfect sense if you consider that if there were an infinite series of utterers and interpreters, there will always be an interpreter downstream of every utterer, and an utterer upstream of every interpreter. Expression still hinges on the individual, at each successive utterance. All along the beginningless and endless line, the movement of thought remains a dual affair between individual utterers and interpreters. Rather than opening expression, this in fact only closes it down all the more exhaustively by infinitizing the centrality of the individual subject. Expression is endlessly imprisoned in the interiority of the speaking subject. If, on the other hand, the collection of utterers and interpreters is finite, then there are loose ends. There is a cut-off point where an utterer's enunciation fails to find an interpreter and falls into the gaps – which is the same thing as an interpretation remaining in potential with no one yet to pass it down the line. Cesura. "If a sign has no interpreter, its interpretant is a *'would be'*, i.e. it is what would determine the interpreter if there was one" (Peirce 1998: 409). A would-be determination of an interpreter: a potential expression. In-forming. *The opening of expressive potential is predicated on the finitude of the collection of utterers.* Expression is no longer a dual affair. It is opened to a "Thirdness," and the third is potential.[3]

The idea of an endless series of utterers and interpreters infinitely displaces the notion of the origin. But an autonomy of expression does not come from the mere absence of the origin. It comes from the affirmation of an absolute origin, at loose ends. As the technique of speed dating makes palpable, this is where potential is to be found: in the gaps in expression and in the threads left hanging. The infinitization of the series of utterers and interpreters actually ends up de-potentializing expression. The farther along the infinite line, the harder it becomes to imagine that there could be anything new left to say or think, as the series reaches closer and closer to the ideal limit where every possible permutation has been exhausted. Even though this limit is ideal, in that it can never actually be reached, the very idea of this infinity of chatter is exhausting. Rather than buoying one with a sense of the richness of variation, it bludgeons one with the sinking feeling of the exhaustion of novelty. What Peirce is inoculating us against is mistaking the openness of thought for an ideal infinity of utterance, and confusing the origin of expression with the beginning of a series (rather than a seriating rebeginning).[4]

What is the "ingredient" of thought-expression that Peirce says comes to the fore when the collection of interlocutors is finite and the reality of signs without utterers or interpreters affirms itself? What can go without an utterer or an interpreter, functioning as "a sort of substitute for them" that fulfills "nearly the same, but more essential, function," at the loose ends of thought-expression?

This essential ingredient, as regards the utterer, is what Peirce calls the "Object" of the sign that constitutes an utterance and enacts an expressive movement of thought through it. This is a peculiar notion of an object. The usual connotations of the word must be bracketed. Here, "object" is really just another word for the meaning or sense of the sign: what the sign "stands for." This standing-for is not to be taken as a synonym for "represent." It must be taken more strongly, as in "take the place of" and even "bear," "carry," or "endure." For rather than being what the sign expresses, the sense/Object of the utterance is actually what goes "necessarily *unexpressed* in the sign" (Peirce 1998: 407).

The sense, Peirce explains, can only come from "a *collateral* source" (404). It is incumbent in the surrounding situation: the situation itself, not as it is represented in the mind of the utterer or the interpreter. It is precisely for the mind of the individual utterer or interpreter – the interiority of his or her thinking – that the Object functions as a more essential substitute. The idea that sense is sourced in the situation collateral to the sign brings thought out into the environment. In *What is Philosophy?* Deleuze and Guattari speak of the work of art as "standing up" (Deleuze and Guattari 1994: 164). By this they mean that what it expresses has its own reality, independent of how the work was pictured in the mind of the artist and how it is received in the mind of its audience. What it expresses has the status of a "being of sensation" or a "block of sensation" to which the work gives standing in the world. Suzanne Langer uses the oxymoron "objective feeling" to get at much the same idea about the import of art (Langer 1953: 19-20). All signs "stand for" in the same way that a configuration of signs composing an artwork "stands up." A sign's sense/Object is a being of thought, a block of thinking:

an *objective contemplation* given standing in the world through its utterance.[5]

A "block" of thinking is not a simple unity. It stands for many. Peirce takes the verb as the privileged example for understanding how signs stand, fully aware of the implications this choice has for our understanding of the nature of the sign-process that is thought-expression ("semiosis"). By privileging the verb, Peirce is asserting that semiosis must be approached on the model of the event. A verb, he says, does not designate particular things. It designates a set of *"partial objects."* These are not in the first instance objects in the everyday sense. They are *roles* composing the event that the verb stands for. The verb "runs" designates a *some*one who embodies a running. The verb "gives" designates a *some*one who proffers, a *some*one who receives, and a *some*thing that passes between them. Both verbs are one word – but stand for more than one, for a *some* composing the action. Their object is unspecified. In the abstract, there are an infinite number of runners, and an infinite series of givers, giftees, and gifts. But neither verb is ever used in the abstract, in the sense of lacking a surrounding situation, whatever, whenever, or wherever that situation may be. The sense of the utterance is never purely general. It is never the infinity of objects that might answer to it generally, in the abstract. The sense of the utterance is the suggestion that there will be someones or somethings in the situation indicated that embody the roles that the event for which the verb stands is wanting. Precisely which ones those are unspecified by the verb. The verb's utterance kick-starts the process of thought-expression by substituting itself for them: it is in the verb's inability to specify precisely which objects are wanting that its sign-power resides. It leaves them to be determined by the situation. The sign *points to* their specification. It stands for what actions may come next that leads to their determination. The power of the sign is to *determine a process of determination* to take place. The process of determination must move collaterally into the situation of the utterance – toward where it points – and supplement the utterance with follow-on actions. Thus, the power of the sign is pragmatic. The essay in which this discussion of Peirce's is found is entitled, simply, "Pragmatism."

A sign does not impress an abstract meaning on the mind. More fundamentally, it poses a *question* to the situation. *Some*: someone, something. But *which* one(es)? The sign points not to a thing, but to an event which it "directs us to seek" (Peirce 1998: 406). The verb powers this collateral action of seeking (what Peirce terms "collateral observation"). The sign's sense – its meaning, import, enunciative *force* – is none other than this powering of an expressive movement inviting a relay into collateral observation and an embodied movement of exploration supplementing the action of the verb.

The Object of the sign is the *"quaesitum"* ("that which must be sought;" Peirce 1998: 406). The quaesitum is the terminus of the expressive movement that orients the process powered by the sign. It is an attractor pole lying at the limit of the movement of sense-making – semiosis, the movement of thought-expression – but at the same time dynamizes it from within, as that toward which the movement tends. It exerts a formative force on the process, operating immanently to it.

As immanent formative force of the movement of thought-expression, the quaesitum is the *"requaesitum"* ("essential ingredient;" Peirce 1998, 404) of making-sense. This Object of the sign is necessarily unexpressed in the sign because it is realized through the unfolding of the process that the sign powers into motion. It is effectively created by the movement of thought actively tending toward it. It is all of this – this unfolding toward a realized fulfillment – that the sign "stands for." It for all of this that it substitutes itself at the inception of the process set in motion by that very standing-for. It is this – the insistence of quaesitum as the necessary ingredient to be sought for –that the sign bears, that is process carries, endures. In short, the Object of the sign is unspecified in the abstract in order to be determinable by process.

Seek – and you may not find. There may be no requisite runner present in the situation, or even anywhere in existence.[6] However, the verb still functions expressively. It "expresses" a process in the sense of "forcing out (as the juice of a fruit) by pressure" (Merriam-Webster). To pressurize the process of thought-expression, the sign doesn't need an actual object. All that is requisite is a quaesitum, a that-which-must-be-sought juicy enough to whet the appetite: a *"would-be"* terminus; an attractor taking upon itself, in the form of its being sought, the sign's expressive force. Would-be: the Object of thought-expression points to the *conditional*. Conditional: of the order of potential. That, finally, is the essential ingredient. *Potential* – determined to be determined (to paraphrase another Peircean formulation[7]) by a process moving thought out, under the pressure of the situation.

When an actual thing is found to fulfill the role of the verb's some/ones or some/things, the process still does not end. Termini are slippery things. The question "which?" just sets the stage for the follow-up question *what else*? What else was required for the required determination to be fulfilled? What more is there that would even more determinately determine the sense of the sign –for example by filling in details or filling out its background? Or by specifying how it plays its role in the event. In what manner is the what-else co-determining of what happens? Thus it is not simply a question of some/ones or some/things being actually present or not. It is also the *way* in which they are present, or would have been. Peirce insists that the Object of thought-expression as quaesitum is necessarily *"singular*, not general." The Object, when there actually is one, is not general, but neither is it a particular this-here. It is this-here-*in-this-way*, along with all else that made it so – and would potentially have made it otherwise. What else? is not a controllable question. It is "impossible to complete our collateral observation" (Peirce 1998: 409). Where does the seeking stop? Between every two would-be this-heres there potentially lies another. At the limit, "there is a continuum between them." The Object, *though singular, may nevertheless be multiple, and may even be infinitely so*" (408; emphasis added).

Is this not a contradiction? The whole discussion started with the problem that where there is an infinity of utterers and interpreters, the movement of expression comes to a halt, exhausted by the very thought of itself. Yet now we've what-elsed and in-what-mannered our way back to infinity. The difference is that this new infinity at which we have arrived is in no way a purely abstract or ideal infinity. It is infinite "in completed existence" (Peirce 1998: 408). It is a *potential infinity* that is pragmatically inscribed in the situation. It is an *effective* infinity, because it *does*: it demands more seeking; it calls for and enables collateral action.[8] It is in no way general, but singularly ingredient to the situation. It is the more-than *of* the situation. It will never be exhausted, try as we might to seek it out. To avoid exhausting ourselves, at some point we will just have to call it quits. We have to deem our collateral observation sufficient to what is Objectively required by the situation for it to terminate itself, for all pragmatic intents and purposes, so that life may move on to a new situation and expression to a new iteration.

It is important to note that this effective infinity is on the side of the environmentality of the Object, not of the individuality of the subject. It is just as important to bear in mind that it overspills any dual relation, being a question of an always-another in between: a third. This *thirdness* interposes itself between the subjects involved, over-filling the gaps between their utterances. It is also what is left over and above the finitude of the individual subjects involved in the situation. It is what exceeds them, so that there must be a sign without an utterer or an interpreter – and, substituting for them, something essential for thought's moving-out pragmatically into process. The something essential that may substitute for the individual subject of expression is all that is potentially sought for collaterally. It is the Object of expression that can never be fully expressed, but without which expression would have nowhere to go but into generality. It is the Object as incumbent in the texture of the situation, replete with would-bes: *all* that is potentially sought for collaterally to "some" up the situation. An all surrounding the some of the sign: the Object become *environmental*, operating throughout an expanded field. The essential ingredient, the "Object," is what Peirce calls the environmental *"form of fact"* (Peirce 1998: 408). It is the all-around of the in-situation, as triangulated by potential.

Once again, Peirce models his pragmatic account of signs and the thought-expression on the verb. As the model verb, he chooses "expresses." "Expresses" is a very special verb. At the same time as it expresses something, he says, it *"expresses its expressing something"* (Peirce 1998: 408). It is self-reporting. But just as the oneness of a verb like "gives" envelops a some, a manyness of roles and potential objects, "expresses" envelops many a verb. In fact, it wraps itself up in all of them, and swaddles them all. For is not "expresses" of the nature of all verbs? Of all signs? Is "expresses" not the natural environment of signs? Do they not, each and every one, have an expressive dimension of self-reporting to them? Is it not through the pressure of the self-reporting of their standing-for that the form-of-fact of their situation comes Objectively to express *itself* through the would-bes and collateral action with which it pragmatically supplements the sign?

Looked at this way, the "partial objects" of the sign's utterance are in form-of-fact *partial subjects* of the process of thought-expression powered by the sign. They collectively self-report through that process's playing out. Peirce says that the utterer and interpreter are "inessential" because the pragmatic "fact" of the situation can substitute for them, in the form of the partial subjects collaterally pressured into, and clamoring, to self-report – and through their self-reporting, potentially bringing the all of the situation to expression. Emphasis, again, on "potentially." The Object is essentially speculative. As self-reporting, the factual form of its infinity is all but one with the Subject of expression, environmentally wrapped up in the situation processually swaddling the requisite would-be somes.

It is important to note that a slippage has occurred in the Peirce terms of this discussion. The analysis imperceptibly transitioned from a something more essential that can fulfill the role of the utterer (the Object) to the corresponding something more essential that can fulfill the role of the interpreter: what Peirce calls the interpretant. Technically, the Object is what in-forms the sign's utterance and orients the movement of thought-expression it inaugurates. The Object is what the sign stands-for. The interpretant, for its part, is what the sign stands-toward: this same Object transformed by the action of the sign into a sought-for terminus. The transition occurs at the quaesitum, which is the Object as *necessarily* sought in the situation. The Object, as that which in-forms the sign and orients the movement of thought-expression it triggers, has the force of an imperative: it necessarily imposes itself on situation at the utterance of the sign. The interpretant is this same imperative turned into a conditional, a would-be: as what, necessarily sought, *may be* found.[9]

The Object and interpretant are strictly complementary. They reciprocally presuppose each other as indissociable aspects of the same process.[10] They relay other in the quaesitum, which is like a gear-shift mechanism or hinge between their respective modes. They overlap in the quaesitum, allowing for a smooth transition and imperceptible transformation from the mode of the imperative to the conditional. The Object prefigures the interpretant, and the interpretant reprises the Object.

They are interwound as inseparable pulses in the playing out of the same tendency to sense-making. It was by virtue of their reciprocal presupposition as indissociable aspects of the process of thought-expression's playing-out that the foregoing discussion was able to segue imperceptibly from the Object to the interpretant. Peirce insists on their logical difference and real distinction, as different aspects. But he also goes out of his way to specify that the interpretant – counter to virtually every secondary interpretation of it in the literature – does *not* have to be "a modification of consciousness" (Peirce 1998: 411). After all, the would-bes of a situation are as much a part of its reality as the imperatives it harbors. The modification of the consciousness of an individual interpreter is not required. All that is required is "a sufficiently close analogue of a modification of consciousness" (411).

This means that the transition from the Object to the interpretant is not, as it is too often made out to be, a transition from the objective in the usual sense to the subjective as normally understood. Something else entirely is at stake: that "the minds of the utterer and the interpreter have to be *fused* in order that any communication should take place" (Peirce 1998: 478; emphasis added). This Peirce enigmatically names the *Commind* (*commens*). It "consists of that which is, and must be, well understood between the utterer and the interpreter, at the outset, in order that the sign in question should fulfill its function" (478). In light of Peirce's statements that the utterer and interpreter are inessential, this definition needs to be amended to: the commind "consists of that which is, and must be, well understood between the utterer and the interpreter, should they be present, or at points where the process does not recede collaterally into the gaps or come to loose ends ..." Elsewhere it is more vaguely understandable. Even where there is a well-understanding utterer and interpreter, the Commind is not just "what is forced upon the mind in perception, but includ[es] *more than perception reveals*" (478). This more-than can only be all the more so in the gaps of potential into which perception's seek its would-be interpretants. So when Peirce says "between" the utterer and interpreter it has to be taken in the strongest sense, as involving the continuum potentially inhabiting the gaps in the situation into which the quaesitum recedes. This effectively extends the Commind well beyond what is "well understood" at the outset, into the processual more-than of the situation: to the partial objects that are also partial subjects. The Commind exceeds the individual subject of perception by nature. It shades into the more-than of the situation's immanent all – where it is always and in any case "already virtually present" (Peirce 1998: 403). It fuses not only utterers and interpreters, should they be present; more-than that, it fuses the effective infinity of partial objects and partial subjects on the continuum of potentially completed existence filling the situation. In the Commind, the Object of expression becomes all but one with a collective (commensal) Subject that is irreducibly environmental. It is this all-in-and-around of the situation that virtually thinks itself, always. In every case, it is essentially the situation's virtual thinking of itself that self-reports through the process of semiosis.

To my knowledge, the Commind occurs in Peirce's implausibly voluminous work exactly once. It is the minorest of all Peircean concepts, the one he left in tendency out of "despair of making my own broader conception understood" (Peirce 1998: 478). To follow through on its tendency is to produce a Peirce more Peircean than Peirce, and hopefully all the more faithful to Peirce for that (in the same way that Deleuze remained faithful to Bergson). This is not just a matter of exegesis of interest to the hermetic society of Peirce hounds. It has tremendous import for the theory of signs and expression, for all of semiotics and all that has come out of it. It turns the normative readings of Peirce that largely informed the construction of late-twentieth-century semiotics on their environmental heads by asserting the absolute necessity of a theory – and a practice – of collective expression. It also underlines the impossibility of representation as a foundational category for thought-expression. The same reasoning that led Peirce to the Commind requires that the interpretant (the sign's fulfilled sense) "does not correspond" to the Object (whose imperative in-forming powers the sense-making process; Peirce 1998: 410). This is because, although they are reciprocally presupposing processual complements that cannot actually be dissociated, the object and the interpretant have different logical status and by virtue of that are really distinct.[11] The "defect of correspondence" is rooted in the "essential difference to their natures" (410): the fact that one is in the imperative that coincides with the triggering of the process by the sign (and is thus left in the past by its unfolding), while the other is in the "relatively future tense" of the conditional (410).[12] For both of these reasons – Commind and the essential defect of representational theories of the sign – speed dating with the ghost of Peirce is sure to be challengingly mind-bending, and is highly recommended.

A final note: it is arbitrary, if instructive, to use parts of speech, such as verbs, in order to model the process of expression, as was done earlier. But of course not every sign is linguistic. A gesture is a nonlinguistic sign. A gesture involves seeings, perhaps touchings, definitely kinesthetic feelings. The interpretant (Commind) "in all cases, includes feelings" along with "something that may vaguely be called 'thought'" (Peirce 1998: 409). Vaguely, because the process of thought-expression Objectively seeks its own would-be fulfillment, which it cannot clearly or distinctly know until it reaches its terminus. However, ninety-nine times out of a hundred (to quote James; 1996: 69) the terminus is *not* reached, so that the process must continue virtually. Or, it will just have to call it quits in the interests of moving on to a next iteration, across a cesura filled with the resonation of many potential lines of thought jostling each other, vying for self-fulfilling what-elses, plying the continuum between the partial objects that collaterally self-report as partial subjects and whose infinite fusion composes the Commind. This pragmatic seeking-doing is a vaguely *thinking-feeling,* complexly determined to be determined environmentally, unfolding in the collective, commensal expression that constitutes "actual *Experience*" (Peirce 1998: 478; emphasis in the original). Actual Experience: the virtual thinking-of-itself of the situation coming pragmatically to expression, self-reporting.

Actual experience is the creature of expression's autonomy.

Radical Pedagogy

Conceptual speed dating is a pragmatic technique for staging the autonomy of collective expression within the particular situation of a given, finite group of utterers and interpreters. In the particular context of the SenseLab, it is a technique for would-be collaborators seeking to transduce their encounter with a generative text into improvisational follow-on explorations in other modes than textual, where linguistic expression moves into an intimacy of thinking-feeling with other-sense activity.

The individuals involved in this practice themselves carry collaterals: their moods, habits, technical and social skills, acquired knowledge, any number of things. In fact, an effective infinity of things. These are also partial objects of the thought-expression that occurs, incumbent in their own way in the situation. Whether or not they are sought, whether or not there is a group determination to determine them, they belong to the form-of-fact of the situation and in-form its potential. Whether sought or not, they self-report: in the strategies an individual deploys to negotiates the enabling constraints of the exercise, in particular the time-limit, and how as a function of those strategies the collective movement of thought-expression is inflected. Sought or not, this range of partial objects of expression are partial subjects of enunciation, by virtue of their inflecting the self-reporting of the situation's all. Although they are usually considered factors "internal" to a speaking subject, the technique of speed dating activates them on the same basis as other situational factors that would normally be categorized as "external." In short, speed dating activates what is normally taken as the personal characteristics of the individual participants as a subset of the *environmental factors* in play. This is done in order to *express thought*, in the sense used earlier of forcing thought out, like the juice from a fruit, so that it lubricates the situation where it collectively moves, in all of its dimensions, involving all of its collaterals operating on the same speculatively pragmatic plane: a kind of "flat ontology" of expression in actual experience.

It is a peculiarity of SenseLab *not* to seek these "internal" factors as such. This is a general principle of SenseLab activities, in all their forms-of-fact and phases. To seek these factors would be to *impress* them into the individual: bring them out from their potential environmentality and limit them to the individual subjectivity of the utterer/interpreter. This would be to personalize expression again, at the expense of the infinity of potentiality that the movement of thought-expression is capable of mobilizing if it is pressurized pragmatically in Peirce's speculative sense, through the thirdness of free indirect discourse. At the limit, it is the *process* of free indirect discourse that is the autonomous Subject of expression all but one with the environmental Object of thought extending into potential (Commind). To personalize this process is to diminish the environmental force of the sign-power of semiosis, whose determination to be determined can only be unleashed if the autonomy of that expression is valued, cared for situationally, and tended to transsituationally with technique. The personal is an interiorizing limitation of that autonomy. Vološinov made the point that expression is in any case only ever personal secondarily. The interiority of the individual speaking subject is the result of signs being "inwardly impelled" by specific techniques of power" (Vološinov 1986: 153). In this, he prefigures Foucault's conviction that the interiorization and personalization of the individual subject is the product of certain historically specific strategies of power. To the extent to which we speak in the first person, rather than the unspecified third person of free indirect discourse, we express not our subjective freedom, but the history of the subjection of expression.

It is a key proposition of the SenseLab that the intensest expression is impersonal and collective in the environmental sense glossed in this essay, where "collective" ceases to be a synonym for a collection of individuals to become the sign-function pointing to the effective potential in the situation that exceeds both the individuals in the group and their aggregate number –but cannot come to expression without them, through their finitude. "Collective" in this sense is the quaesitum: that which must be sought in any event of expression if it is to fulfill its Object (in such a way that it pragmatically becomes all but one with the commensal Subject of expression).

Radical pedagogy, for the SenseLab, consists in recognizing this quaesitum as the requaesitum it is: as the essential ingredient for expression to raise itself to its most fully potentialized plane, in a thinking-feeling of the intensest sort. It is the SenseLab's proposition that a radical pedagogy is a collective-seeking that honors the autonomy of expression and tends to its intense impersonality, experimenting with very precise speculative-pragmatic techniques for staging it and caring for its process. This is what sets a radical pedagogy apart from mere learning, and the way the modes of learning dominant in our institutions misconstrue the Object of thought-expression for an object of knowledge to be acquired by an individual subject (impelled by the many limiting powers of subjection structuring contemporary institutions of learning). Radical pedagogy operates in the gaps in knowledge. Its process moves thought-expression collaterally into the unknowns of the situation, where its effectively infinite potential self-reports.

A radical pedagogy:

1. Proceeds rigorously through technique.
2. Uses the technique to jump start an event of expression.
3. Strategizes the jump-starting of the event in such a way as to take up a finite collection of utterers and interpreters in a collective movement of thought.
4. Collateralizes expression so as to bring the situation of the event to singular expression.
5. Brings the situation to singular expression in a way that gives complete existence to the situation's real potential *as* potential, objectively infinite.
6. Is attentive to the manner in which every expression also expresses its own expression, building on that to double the objectively infinite potential of the situation with an expression-of-expression that enables the event to reference its own process, so as to correct, perfect, and vary its own technique.
7. Leaves loose ends, releasing and remaindering potential in a way that it self-forwards across the gaps to a next event in a different mode of practice, relaying the expressive event into situations and techniques beyond itself.
8. Takes this outdoing of itself to be its content, in dogged resistance to any notion of knowledge in terms of a content separable from the event of its own expressive self-production.
9. Transduces rather than transmits.

Notes

1. By Andrew Murphie, during the first international research-creation event the SenseLab hosted, *Dancing the Virtual* (2005).

2. This is a similar feeling to the one described in chapter 2 in the context Tino Sehgal's *This Situation,* which uses a completely different technique, demonstrating that the same effect may be achieved by many different means.

3. "Semiosis" involves a "tri-relative influence" that is "not in any way resolvable into actions between pairs" (Peirce 1998: 411).

4. The subtext here will be clear to readers old enough to remember the general academic discourse of the 1980s and much of the 1990s. The idea of an endless series of utterers and interpreters gained prominence with the poststructuralist concept of intertextuality. Postmodernism took on board the logical consequences of this concept, in its ironic affirmation of the sinking feeling of the exhaustion of novelty, accompanied by the refrain of the impossibility of creativity. A compensatory discourse of appropriation and remix emerged. But it was not enough to save the strands of poststructuralism embracing intertextuality and its digital culture equivalent, hypertextuality, from postmodernism's carrying of it to its logical conclusion.

5. Since artworks are compositions of signs, this means that their objective feeling envelops thought: that they are thinking-feelings presenting with the feeling standing out. Conversely, all signs composing what we call thinking as opposed to feeling, envelop feelings, with the thinking standing for.

6. There are of course many uses of language – the vast majority, in fact – where there is no assumption of the physical presence of the Object of expression. The ability of language to function in situations where the Object as it might figure in the immediate situation is absent is, as is so often pointed out, what gives language its vast powers of expression. Peirce's point is that when this is case, there is still seeking – but one that remains in the register of potential. The follow-on actions are performed virtually. It is in order to make this point that Peirce emphasizes that a thought is sign for another thought ("every thought beyond immediate perception is a sign;" Peirce 1998: 402). Everything that applies to situations assuming the possible presence of

the object applies to the virtual situations of thought operating directly in its natural environment of potential. Even the seemingly contextless examples of analytic philosophers and logicians, like the infamous cat on the mat, are not entirely without an appeal to a situation (is the cat on the mat because it wants to exit the door, or is it just taking a nap?). But more importantly than this abstract context (in the sense of being without pragmatic stakes) is the context of the enunciation. A discussion of an abstract cat on a mat is a concrete demonstration belonging to a genre of language (philosophy) that carries institutional weight. The stakes of the enunciation itself are all the more weighty the more distant the Object of expression. These stakes include the assertion or imposition of the genre of expression to which the utterance signs its participation, the institutional associated with that genre, the informal factors associated with the particularities of the situation of the enunciation, and the way in which all of these factors position the speaker and give authority or performative efficacy to his or her utterance. The dimension of "self-reporting" (discussed below) that is an element of every utterance becomes all the more pronounced here, to the point that under certain circumstances it becomes the equivalent of the self-presentation that the technique of speed dating attempts to side-step, even if that gesture is not explicitly performed. That is why it is crucial for practices like the SenseLab's to create open situations of unspecified potential that support collateral action without directing it advance, and that foreground the collectivity of expression, while avoiding general statements.

7. "Potential means indeterminate yet capable of determination. ... The vague always tends to become determinate, simply because its vagueness does not determine it to be vague. ... It is not determinately nothing" (Peirce, 1998: 323-324).

8. The distinction being made here between a general or purely abstract infinity (what Peirce calls a "hypothetical infinite collection") and and an effective infinity pragmatically inscribed in a situation (thus having what Peirce calls an infinity having "completed existence") corresponds to Whitehead's distinction between "pure potential" and "real potential." Real potential is "indetermination, rendered determinate in the real concrescence ... it is a conditioned indeterminacy" (Whitehead 1978: 23; see also 65-66). The demand that real potential makes for a process of thought-expression

seeking to determine it is what Whitehead calls the "proposition" (1978: 184-207).

9. The Object is singular. The interpretant, on the other hand, is "either general or intimately connected with generals" (Peirce 1998: 410). A general would-be is a possibility. The transformation from imperative to conditional is associated with a *transformation of potential into possibility*. This linking of potential to the imperative – the requaesitum – and the idea that *possibility is produced*, derived from the imperative movement of potenital, is a significant shift in the way we normally think of these categories, with even more significant implications for how we conceive of freedom. In terms of the earlier discussion of generality in this essay, it is when possibility is disconnected from its derivation in potential that the plane of the general seems to take on independence from situation and process, and assert its claims to abstract self-sufficiency. The lesson is not that generality is not useful or is not produced; it is, rather, that *generality is always produced as a phase-shift of singularity*.

10. As is the case with Peirce's triadic categories of Firstness/Secondness/Thirdness, and icon/index /symbol which are similarly mutually participating processual complements that cannot be dissociated from each other.

11. A real distinction, as employed by Deleuze, is a distinction that is "essential or qualitative" but non-numerical (cannot be parsed out as belonging to different substantially different things) (Deleuze 1994: 40). Peirce's triadic categories are similarly real distinctions.

12. See also their difference as regards singularity and generality discussed in note 9.

Works Cited

Ayache, Elie. 2010. *The Blank Swan: The End of Probability*. Chichester: Wiley.

Bergson, Henri. 1998. *Creative Evolution*. Trans. Arthur Miller. Mineola, NY: Dover.

Bryan, Dick and Michael Rafferty. 2006. *Capitalism with Derivatives: A Political Economy of Financial Derivatives, Capital and Class*. New York: Palgrave-Macmillan.

Chion, Michel. 1994. *Audio-Vision: Sound on Screen*. Trans. Claudia Gorbman. New York: Columbia University Press.

Deleuze, Gilles. 1994. *Difference and Repetition*. Trans. Paul Patton. New York: Columbia University Press.

Deleuze, Gilles. 1995. "Postscript on the Society of Control." In *Negotiations*. Trans. Martin Joughin. New York: Columbia University Press, 177-182.

Deleuze, Gilles and Félix Guattari. 1983. *Anti-Oedipus*. Trans. Robert Hurley, Mark Seem, and Helen R. Lane. Minneapolis: University of Minnesota Press.

Deleuze, Gilles and Félix Guattari. 1987. *A Thousand Plateaus*. Trans. Brian Massumi. Minneapolis: University of Minnesota Press.

Deleuze, Gilles and Félix Guattari. 1994. *What is Philosophy?* Trans. Graham Burchell and Hugh Tomlinson. London: Verso.

Economic Space Agency (ECSA). http://ecsa.io.

Foucault, Michel. 1977. *Discipline and Punish: Birth of the Prison*. Trans. Alan Sheridan. New York: Pantheon.

Guattari, Felix. 2014. *The Three Ecologies*. Trans. Ian Pindar and Paul Sutton. London: Bloomsbury.

James, William. 1996. *Essays in Radical Empiricism*. Lincoln: University of Nebraska Press.

Langer, Susanne. 1953. *Feeling and Form: A Theory of Art*. New York: Charles Scribner's Sons.

Lee, Benjamin and Randy Martin, eds. 2016. *Derivatives and the Wealth of Societies*. Chicago: University of Chicago Press.

Manning, Erin. 2009. *Relationscapes: Movement, Art, Philosophy*. Durham, NC: Duke University.

Manning, Erin. 2016. *The Minor Gesture*. Durham, NC: Duke University.

Manning, Erin and Brian Massumi. 2014. *Thought in the Act: Passages in the Ecology of Experience*. Minneapolis: University of Minnesota Press.

Massumi, Brian. 2011. *Semblance and Event: Activist Philosophy and the Occurrent Arts*. Cambridge, MA: MIT Press.

Massumi, Brian. 2014a. *The Power at the End of the Economy*. Durham, NC: Duke University.

Massumi, Brian. 2014b. *What Animals Teach Us about Politics*. Durham, NC: Duke University.

Massumi, Brian. 2015. *Ontopower: War, Powers, and the State of Perception*. Durham, NC: Duke University.

Massumi, Brian. 2017. "Virtual Ecology and the Question of Value." In *General Ecology: The New Ecological Paradigm*. Ed. Erich Hörl. London: Bloomsbury. 345-373.

Moten, Fred and Stefano Harney. 2013. *The Undercommons: Fugitive Planning and Black Study*. New York: Minor Compositions.

Moore, Jason W. 2015. *Capitalism in the Web of Life: Ecology and the Accumulation of Capital*. London: Verso.

Nietzsche, Friedrich. 2003. *Writings from the Late Notebooks*. Ed. Rüdiger Bittner. Trans. Kate Sturge. Cambridge: Cambridge University Press.

Peirce, Charles S. 1998. *The Essential Peirce: Selected Philosophical Writings*, vol. 2. Bloomington: University of Indiana Press.

Russell, Bertrand. 1996. *The History of Western Philosophy*. London: Routledge.

SenseLab. http://senselab.ca.

Simondon, Gilbert. 1969. *Du mode d'existence des objets techniques*. Paris: Aubier-Montagne.

Vološinov, V.N. 1986. *Marxism and the Philosophy of Language*. Trans. Ladislav Matejka and I.R. Titunik. Cambridge, MA: Harvard University Press.

Whitehead, Alfred North. 1967. *Adventures of Ideas*. New York: Free Press.

Whitehead, Alfred North. 1978. *Process and Reality*. New York: Free Press.

Williams, Alex and Nick Srnicek. 2014. "#Accelerate: Manifesto for an Accelerationist Politics." In *#Accelerate*. Ed. Robin MacKay and Armen Avanessian. Falmouth: Urbanomic. 347-362.